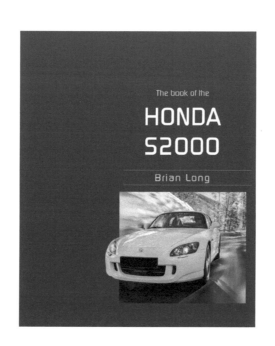

The book of the

HONDA
S2000

Brian Long

T0386305

Discover more from Veloce's other imprints, featuring a wide range of general interest, animal care and children's books

www.veloce.co.uk

First published in December 2020 by Veloce Publishing Limited, Veloce House, Parkway Farm Business Park, Middle Farm Way, Poundbury, Dorchester DT1 3AR, England. This paperback edition printed March 2021.
Tel +44 (0)1305 260068 / Fax 01305 250479 / e-mail info@veloce.co.uk / web www.veloce.co.uk or www.velocebooks.com
ISBN: 978-1-787117-51-8; UPC: 6-36847-01751-4

The book of the
HONDA
S2000

Brian Long

VELOCE PUBLISHING
THE PUBLISHER OF FINE AUTOMOTIVE BOOKS

Contents

Introduction
& acknowledgements

The Honda S2000 came into our lives at an awkward moment – too late to make the most of the lightweight sports car (LWS) boom created by open cars like the Mazda MX-5, and a victim of the financial crisis that followed in the wake of the Lehman shock. Why is it, then, that so many enthusiasts have fond memories of this short-lived machine, and why is it seemingly even more popular today? Hopefully, the pages that follow – illustrated with contemporary material throughout to aid those looking for authenticity – will help explain why the S2000 was always special, as we cover the car's development, its launch in 1999, and its incredibly convoluted evolution through to its demise in 2009, taking a look at all the major markets along the way. Covering the JDM, US, European and Australian markets is the norm for this author when it comes to writing about Japanese cars, and as you'll see, it was necessary with this model, otherwise nothing would make sense, especially in view of there being so many grey imports around nowadays.

Before we start, those hoping for in-depth coverage of the tuning side of things will be disappointed – as a darling with tuners and custom shops, the subject is just too vast, and besides, buyers today are far more interested in originality. Knowing what is and what isn't correct for a certain year is far more important than pages full of bits of carbon-fibre and strange wheels, and, believe me, just sorting that out is a nightmare. Parts offered by Honda (or Mugen) are a different matter, of course, and these are detailed as we go along.

As always, books like this cannot be put together without the help of the factory. Yukiko Watanabe is my main contact there nowadays, and it is her we must thank for filling in the gaps in my tons of material gathered during decades of shows, launches and interviews. Regular trips to the JMIF Library in Tokyo put the finishing touches on a few things, and Kenichi Kobayashi at Miki Press was as helpful as ever. In amongst the cast of dozens of supporting members (not least, my long-suffering wife, acting, as always, as the in-house translator), there's another important angle that readers tend to forget about – having friends behind you to provide the encouragement needed to keep you going. In that respect, I am blessed in having people like Simon Pickford in my corner. Simon, as a proud S2000 owner, this one is for you …

Brian Long
Chiba City, Japan

A brief history
of Honda

Always innovative, the Honda company has long been associated with racing and sporting machinery. Before going on to look at the main subject of this book – the S2000 – it is worth taking a few moments to reflect on Honda's history, for it helps to put the project into perspective.

The story of Honda is rooted in one man's dream to get Japan mobile again following the devastation of World War Two. Left with little in the way of resources following constant heavy bombing by wave after wave of B-29s, and the desire to keep the Imperial war machine going in a long and bitter fight, the Occupying Forces ensured that what little industry *did* survive was disbanded in order to weaken its position; Japan was going to have to start from ground zero.

The Japan of 1945 was hardly recognisable compared to that country five years earlier, at least in the cities. Most of the houses were constructed using wood, to better withstand earthquakes, but firebombs made short work of these vulnerable structures; conventional bombs destroyed much of the country's factories, as well as the road and rail networks, and raw materials were in short supply.

It took a long time to convert the remaining factories to enable them to produce goods needed to rebuild the infrastructure, and any thought of personal transport, other than a bicycle, was usually scotched by the excessive cost of motorised vehicles. Imported machines were very expensive, and domestic producers tended to concentrate on light commercials and two-wheelers, knowing full well that few people were in a position to buy a car – assuming they had the capacity to build one in the first place! In fact, even scooters and motorcycles were fairly costly, due to high inflation in the immediate post war years. It was against this background, however, that the seeds were sown for what would grow into a massive empire with manufacturing plants in every corner of the world.

A DREAM

Soichiro Honda was born on 17 November 1906 in Yamahigashi, a country village a few miles to the west of Mount Fuji, and nowadays a Tenryu Ward suburb of Hamamatsu City. The son of a blacksmith and skilled artisan, he grew up with a love for all things mechanical and electrical, and had a deep enthusiasm for automobiles and aeroplanes.

Honda's passion for cars came from a childhood experience, when as a young boy one rumbled past him. Legend has it that he ran after the machine, taking in the

Soichiro Honda (1906-1991). For his sterling work in the motor industry around the world, Honda was rightfully inducted into the Automotive Hall of Fame in Detroit in 1989, and the Japanese version (JAHFA) as soon as inductions began in 2001.

smell of the exhaust, and even stopping to touch a patch of oil that it had left in the road. He was hooked, and vowed that one day he would make his own horseless carriage, just like the one he'd seen.

Meanwhile, the young Honda helped his father, Gihei, in the family workshop, crafting and repairing everything from guns and swords to bicycles. As the years passed, the family business moved further and further toward the cycle trade, Gihei Honda even going so far as to teach the locals how to ride in order to increase sales.

After Soichiro graduated from school in 1922, he was accepted as an apprentice at Art Shokai, an exclusive automobile repair shop in Tokyo. He soon became disillusioned with the menial tasks he was given, however, but refused to quit before acquiring the skills he so desperately wanted to learn. In this difficult period, he found solace in an adjoining workshop, which housed one of Japan's earliest racing cars. He would go there in the evening, and watch the mechanics working away on this Daimler-engined machine.

Ironically, Honda's life changed for the better after the Great Kanto earthquake. He learnt how to drive, as he was required to move cars, and became a proficient motorcycle rider. And while most of the staff went back to their homes outside Tokyo, as the main workshop was virtually destroyed, Honda stayed on and got to work on the racer that had survived the massive quake in the other premises.

The racing car project progressed slowly initially, but the old Buick chassis was replaced by a Mitchell one, and the straight-six Daimler unit was dropped in favour of a Curtiss V8 aero-engine. On its debut, Honda was in the passenger seat as a riding mechanic, and it duly won its maiden outing. Racing was now a big part of Honda's life, and as business returned to pre-disaster levels, his skills as an engineer became quite extraordinary for a man of his age. After six years in Tokyo, he was given permission to open his own branch of Art Shokai in Hamamatsu, close to his birthplace.

A FRESH CHALLENGE

The Hamamatsu branch of Art Shokai opened in April 1928. Business was slow at first, but Honda soon built up a good reputation, and, within a year, had 15 employees working full-time. However, most of his money was earned through royalties on the cast iron wheel spokes he'd patented, and the success of this invention allowed

him to lead the life of a playboy by the time the 1930s rolled along.

Honda quickly became bored with this lifestyle, though, and needed a challenge on which to focus his attention. He decided to go into the piston ring manufacturing business, but for several years this was an unsuccessful venture that drained him physically, emotionally and financially. Even an attempt to brighten his outlook on life via a new racing car ended in disaster after it crashed on its maiden outing, putting both Soichiro and his brother in hospital. Eventually, after taking several lengthy courses at Technical College, he was able to refine the composition of his piston rings, and was back on track. Tokai Seiki Jyukogyo, as the piston ring company was called, ultimately became a subsidiary of the growing Toyota empire.

With the Manchuria occupation and the onset of World War Two, supplying the needs of the military made Honda wealthy once more, whilst his active mind helped refine production methods. Among other things, he invented an automatic propeller cutting machine, earning him an advisory position at Nippon Gakki – the Hamamatsu firm that later became Yamaha. By the end of the conflict, though, Honda had sold his remaining shares in Tokai Seiki to Toyota, and was left with plenty of time on his hands to consider his next plan of action.

THE EARLY POSTWAR YEARS

After a year in the wilderness, Honda duly returned to what he knew and loved: establishing a research laboratory called Honda Gijyutsu Kenkyujo in Hamamatsu. The premises were far from grand, being the bombed-out remains of one of the Tokai Seiki factories, but Honda's hopes were high as Japan faced up to the challenge of rebuilding itself.

Eventually, Honda came up with the idea of using a small 50cc engine used by the military to power a bicycle to provide a cheap form of personal transport; it proved very popular. With a shortage of suitable materials, Honda adopted the old-style Japanese hot water bottle as a fuel tank, and around 500 were built before stocks of the original generator engine ran out. Encouraged by the brisk sales of these rather Heath Robinson-like machines, the Honda Motor Co Limited was founded in September 1948 to produce a new two-stroke engine to power a new motorbike. The 50cc Type A was duly followed by the Type B and Type

The Type D motorcycle, better known as the Honda Dream.

C, and, by 1949, motorcycle production was up to 1000 units per month.

However, whilst Honda was an inspired engineer, he was not as talented when it came to managing finance. Luckily, a friend introduced him to Takeo Fujisawa, who became the company's MD in October 1949. Fujisawa put the business on a sound footing, with the two men taking it from strength to strength over the ensuing years. The achievements of both Honda and Fujisawa were recently recognised in the Japan Automotive Hall of Fame (JAHFA).

BUSINESS EXPANSION
Honda launched the Type D motorcycle in August 1949. Christened the 'Dream,' this was the first design to integrate the engine (up to 98cc) and frame, and was, as such, a major advance compared to its predecessors. With more than 5000 distributors established due to Fujisawa's work behind the scenes, and the popularity of a cheap, reliable product, company growth was truly staggering, with new production plants being built first in Tokyo, and then neighbouring Saitama, in order to keep up with demand.

The Cub of 1952 was another Honda success story, prompting the purchase of a massive piece of land for an additional factory in Saitama, and a head office move to Tokyo. With phenomenal sales, Honda ploughed the money back into the business to purchase new machinery from Europe and America, allowing

Introduced in the early 1950s, the Honda Cub evolved to provide the standard mode of transport for the masses throughout whole swathes of Asia for decades. This advert is from the tail-end of 1968, although the bike's design is similar to the Super Cub of a decade earlier.

Jim Redman (left), Luigi Taveri and Kunimitsu Takahashi at the 1963 Dutch TT. (Courtesy Dutch National Archives, Jack de Nijs/Anefo)

greater productivity, which would ultimately increase profits in the long-term. The timing could have been better, though, as the end of the Korean War brought about an acute recession. Fortunately, investment from the Mitsubishi Bank got Honda through this difficult period, allowing loans to be repaid, but the first Benly motorcycle and the Juno scooter did not sell well, and left the company floundering again.

It was at this time, in March 1954, that Soichiro Honda came up with a make-or-break decision to enter the prestigious Isle of Man TT Race. Although it would be five years before Honda tackled the famous course,

and a further two before it experienced the sweet smell of success, somehow the company weathered the storm, partly through freshly-opened export markets, partly due to the continued success of Dream and Cub variants, as well as new versions of the Benly.

Honda's gamble ultimately paid off, and the worldwide recognition achieved by a crushing victory in the 125cc and 250cc classes at the TT duly translated into a healthy increase in sales, especially abroad. By now, Honda had its own dedicated R&D facility, a base in Europe (in Germany), another plant at Suzuka, and plans to build a racetrack on the same site.

HONDA AUTOMOBILES

The Suzuka Circuit was completed in September 1962. The following month, when the doors of the Tokyo Show opened, Honda grabbed the domestic headlines with a new range of four-wheelers – the S360, the S500, and the T360 light commercial. Whilst the S360 fell by the wayside, the T360 made it into production, about seven months ahead of the S500 sports car. Powered by a high-revving, four-cylinder, twin-cam engine rated at 44bhp, the S500 was launched in October 1963, and was duly followed by the S600 and S800, the latter going on sale in 1966, the year the front-wheel drive N360 *Kei* was announced.

By now, Japan was enjoying an economic boom and Honda was a household name around the world. A brilliant advertising campaign had stolen the hearts of Americans, Honda motorcycles filled the roads of Asia, and the motorsport-loving Europeans couldn't help but respect Honda for the success of its latest venture – an assault on the world of Formula 1.

Soichiro Honda announced his intentions to join the F1 circus at the S600's launch in January 1964. He was applying the same basic philosophy to cars that he'd used with his motorcycles: racing not only improves the

Soichiro Honda pictured with the RA270 F1 prototype.

breed, it also increases sales if a victory can be secured. Of course, it works both ways, and failure would have spelt doom, but Honda was determined to take up the gauntlet.

The RA270 prototype gave way to the RA271. Making

The Honda S500 sports car of 1963 vintage. This was an accomplished design based on the X170 and X190 prototypes, and a massive step forward for the company. The X190 was particularly interesting, having a glass-fibre body (steel was used for production), and a flat-four engine instead of an all-alloy, in-line unit.

its debut at the 1964 German Grand Prix, the RA271 was Japan's first F1 car, and, whilst this V12 machine was extremely advanced, it was left to the RA272 to claim Honda's first victory, courtesy of Richie Ginther on the

The N360 was Honda's answer to the BMC Mini and Fiat 500. It was far sportier and more entertaining than its European counterparts, despite a tiny engine. This is the larger-engined N600 variant, brought out in 1968.

Right and below: American advertising for the legendary CB750 Four, this piece dating from 1969.

Sooner or later, you knew Honda would do it.

This is the one you knew Honda could produce. And would produce. Because only Honda had the technical skill to make it. This is the big one, Jack. The Honda 750 Four.

A four-cylinder single overhead cam engine, transversely mounted in a sleek double-cradle frame. Four carbs. And four chrome pipes— one for each cylinder—individually tuned to fever pitch. Like when you cover a standing quarter in 12.6 sec.

Honda shelled out plenty in research and development. You better believe it.

This baby was born in Grand Prix competition. And raised in the Honda heritage of power and precision. Delivers 68 hp at 8500 rpm. Hits 125 mph sans coaxing. The transmission is five speed constant mesh. An engineering marvel.

Among the new features: no fade, hydraulic front wheel disc brake. Four upswept megaphone style mufflers. Oil pressure light is housed in the tachometer. New color styles.

Your Honda dealer will have it soon. The Honda 750 Four. When you twist the throttle, remember one thing. You asked for it.

Honda 750 Four

1965 Mexican Grand Prix. Another win came in Italy in 1967 (with John Surtees at the wheel of an RA300), but, with more to lose than gain, that was the year in which Honda announced its withdrawal from motorcycling's jewel in the crown – the TT races – and the F1 programme was cancelled not long after, its purpose served.

A NEW BREED OF HONDA CARS

With the Honda name established and export markets opening up, the company displayed the air-cooled 1300 at the 1968 Tokyo Show, putting the car into production in mid-1969. Air-cooled engines were to be short-lived at Honda, however, as water-cooled units replaced them in the 1300's successor (the H145 model), and the highly successful Civic, an 1169cc machine launched in July 1972.

Air pollution then became a serious environmental issue, and the Muskie Act forced Honda into developing a new, clean power unit to satisfy American regulations. Honda ranked 12th in the US import car league table in 1972, but was set to climb the ladder thanks to its CVCC (Compound Vortex Controlled Combustion) system. The stratified charge CVCC unit literally took the world by storm, and sales of the Civic – with its low emission engine – were very strong in the States. American Honda sales leapt from just over 20,000 units in 1972 to 102,389 three years later when CVCC models filtered through; once the Accord was added for the 1976 season, there was to be no looking back.

Meanwhile, after total motorcycle production reached a staggering 20 million units, Soichiro Honda and Takeo Fujisawa retired in October 1973, leaving the company to a new generation of dyed-in-the-wool Honda men such as Kiyoshi Kawashima, Tadashi Kume and Nobuhiko Kawamoto (Kawashima had been involved with Honda from its earliest

The Honda Z was a fun car based on the N360. Originally powered by an air-cooled engine, later models had water-cooled units.

Domestic advertising for the groundbreaking first generation Civic.

The original Honda Legend. Incidentally, the Legend was sold through the Acura dealer network in the States, established in March 1986 to handle Honda's upmarket models.

As well as an enviable reputation in motorcycle racing, Honda had the right image in the car world, thanks to its links with the McLaren F1 team. Honda's success in this most competitive arm of motorsport (its engines claiming the World Championship in 1986 and 1987 with Williams, and ultimately in 1988, 1989, 1990 and 1991 with McLaren) fully justified the company's launch of a supercar, despite having fielded nothing like it before. This early NSX is featured in a Japanese Polymax car polish advert.

The Honda Beat – a mid-engined lightweight sports car that revived memories of the company's first roadsters, and a model that still enjoys a strong following amongst enthusiasts.

After a great deal of Formula One success, especially when teaming up with McLaren, Honda announced its withdrawal from the F1 scene in 1992. At least Hiro Honda's Mugen outfit continued to represent the family name, supplying engines to the likes of Ligier and Jordan, and Honda USA duly started its Indycar campaign in the 1994 season.

The elegant Honda Prelude from the early 1990s.

days, even designing and testing the first motorcycles; Kume was famous for his work on the CVCC engine, and Kawamoto for his exploits in the competitions department, working alongside Formula 1 icon, Yoshio 'Naka' Nakamura).

The Civic and Accord were joined by the sporty Prelude model for the 1979 season, when annual car production surpassed the 700,000 mark (with US sales accounting for half of this figure). The success of the Honda automobile can perhaps be gauged by the fact that a manufacturing plant was established in the States, the Civic was being built in New Zealand from CKD kits, the UK's British Leyland produced the new Ballade (badged as the Triumph Acclaim) following the first of several technical co-operation deals, and a joint project with Mercedes-Benz building cars with Honda engines, transmissions and bodies was put in motion in South Africa. By 1986, Honda was America's top-selling import car.

Soichiro Honda died on 5 August 1991 at the age

Japanese advertising from 1995 showing the NSX-T.

of 84. Having returned to the F1 scene in 1983, initially supplying engines to Williams for the following season, at least the great man had witnessed Honda's success in Formula 1 in an era where the McLaren-Hondas of Ayrton Senna and Alain Prost dominated the scene, following on from where the Williams-Hondas left off. He saw the upmarket Acura line introduced in America in 1986 (with the Integra and Legend kicking things off for the new brand name), the introduction of the VTEC engine, the launch of the 656cc Beat a few months before his death,

and was on hand to witness the development and first sales of the flagship of the Honda range – the handbuilt 280PS NSX supercar.

Honda had come a long way in a short space of time. It took on and conquered established European motorcycle makers, going from zero to hero – by winning the legendary TT race – in just over a decade, and its successful entry into the highly competitive world of Formula 1 astonished everyone, coming only a year or so on the heels of the first production road car, and at a time when the Japanese motor industry was still largely unknown outside Asia. Sales soared after the energy crisis of the 1970s, and the 1980s brought with them a new luxury line-up and a series of F1 titles. Yet, despite the firm's achievements in the field of competition and an ever-expanding range of respected road cars, Honda had still to make a sports car that would truly reflect the company's exploits on the race track. The NSX was the machine which would set the record straight ...

Announced in the spring of 1989, the aluminium-bodied NSX was powered by a three-litre V6, and was sold as an Acura model in the States from August 1990 – a month before domestic sales began, and half-a-year ahead of most other markets. The car received a huge welcome from the press and public alike, with production reaching just over 8400 units in 1991. Then, of course, the bubble burst. The weathervane that symbolises the boom and bust cycle of the world economy had suddenly turned towards wet and windy, and makers of supercars and other luxury goods were amongst the first to be hit by the storm. Indeed, NSX production dropped to only 1272 units in 1992, and would drop even further in the following year.

Notwithstanding, Nobuhiko Kawamoto (who had been in the President's office since mid-1990, following the retirement of Tadashi Kume) stood firm behind the company's sporting line-up. A Targa version of the NSX was introduced in the spring of 1995 to extend its appeal ahead of a series of major revisions planned for the model in 1997, and the sporty Integra-R reduced the gap between the NSX and its Honda brethren, followed by the Civic Type R in due course.

We could also look forward to a revival of the 'Honda Spirit' now that global recession was officially over, and Honda's business had stabilised, despite the unfavourable trading climate the world's car makers found themselves in. Admitting that the company had played safe during the early 1990s and cut costs wherever possible (such as axing the F1 programme), President Kawamoto went on record at this time as saying: "We would like to re-emphasise Honda's flair for innovation."

Car production hit 30 million units in 1995, and towards the end of the 1995 racing season, Honda claimed its first victory in the Indycar series. In 1996, Honda would win the Indycar title, with Jimmy Vasser securing the drivers' crown thanks to Honda power; another Honda runner, Alex Zanardi, was named 'Rookie of the Year.'

The Honda range was by now a very extensive one. In the States, for instance, US Hondas for 1996 included the Accord, Prelude, Civic, Civic del Sol, Odyssey and Passport. The Acura line-up included an all-new RL and American-made CL, the TL, SLX, Integra and NSX/NSX-T. Meanwhile, on the other side of the Pacific, the SSM convertible concept car was creating something of a buzz at the 1995 Tokyo Show.

The S2000
concept

As we have seen in the opening chapter, the notion of building agile and compact convertibles was hardly a new one for Honda, although one had to go back to the short-lived Beat to find a true example of the LWS breed. With the market suddenly flooded with small open cars, a drophead revival was long overdue in the Honda camp ...

1995 had started badly in Japan. In January, the Great Hanshin Earthquake had rocked Kobe and the surrounding area, killing thousands, and leaving many more injured or homeless. A few weeks later, the Aum Shinrikyo cult carried out a second deadly sarin gas attack, this time on the Tokyo subway system. In the spring, Tokyo announced it was cancelling its high-profile 'World City' exposition on the grounds of escalating costs, and so on. Months passed, and despite falling production (a total of 7,610,000 passenger cars built was the worst figure posted in Japan since 1984), on 28 October, the Tokyo Motor Show opened its doors to the general public with a theme of 'Dream the Dream.' Held at Makuhari Messe in Chiba, bordering Tokyo, the condensed event would hopefully provide folks with a welcome respite from the seemingly endless onslaught of doom and gloom on the domestic news front.

THE 1995 TOKYO MOTOR SHOW
The 31st Tokyo Show played host to a number of

Ticket for the 1995 Tokyo Show.

important automotive debutantes – Mazda's magnificent RX-01, and Toyota's MRJ and Prius prototypes amongst them. Honda's F-MX one-box van was a sad reflection on the direction the industry was about to head in, with plenty of SUVs also indicating future trends. But it was the Honda SSM two-seater roadster that caught the attention of many enthusiasts, with lines showing a tasteful blend of tradition and modernity, and a powertrain that suggested it was a more realistic proposal than many of the other concept cars on display at the bi-annual Chiba gathering.

The SSM (Sports Study Model) was styled in-house by Daisuke Sawai, then in his mid-20s, at Honda's Wako site in the eastern part of Saitama, close to Tokyo's northern edge. It was a futuristic design, but obviously meant to provide a realistic sounding board for Honda's marketing people, with power-units, potential pricing, and even the production location and date being mentioned in the contemporary press following interviews with key members of staff at the show.

The NSX was something special, both in the way it was made and the way it performed, but it was expensive and time-consuming to build, and the price-tag simply propelled it into an exclusive niche market. Aiming for a 1998 release date, the SSM would fight in the mainstream open sports car category, built alongside the NSX at Tochigi, but retailing for around one-third of the price. It would have a steel body to keep costs in check, and be powered by a 2-litre five-cylinder engine mated to a five-speed 'F-Matic' semi-automatic gearbox, like that introduced on the NSX in the spring of 1995, to drive the rear wheels.

It was obvious that Honda had thought things through. The 20v SOHC straight-five, usually found in the Inspire saloon and suchlike, was well-respected, with plenty of tuning potential, but an exotic twin-cam VTEC spec was mooted for the SSM, taking the 160bhp quoted for the 2-litre Inspires and Vigors up to a heady output of 200bhp for the same displacement. However, this powerplant was not found in any other Honda, and the five-cylinder G-series family was about to be ditched anyway, so, in reality, it's unlikely to exist outside the promotional video made for the concept car. Indeed, the cam cover is all that is ever shown, rather than a complete engine bay, so one can be fairly sure that a G20A unit was used to make the SSM mobile, and the rest is a myth.

Whatever the engine specification was, with 200bhp almost certainly being a ballpark figure to gauge reaction, the unit was placed as close to the front bulkhead as possible in order to provide the SSM with good weight distribution – a necessity in an FR (front engine, rear-wheel drive) sports car if the handling is to reach the required bench mark standards.

Other features aimed at enhancing the handling were also evident, with a double-wishbone suspension specified all-round, a wide track at both ends, the wheels pushed out to the corners to provide a long-wheelbase and short overhangs, and a weight of just 1100kg (2420lb), achieved thanks to fairly compact dimensions, a spartan interior (with Recaro bucket seats, a digital dashboard, and a longitudinal member that divided the cockpit and helped strengthen the body), as well as the lack of any kind of roof.

Built on a wheelbase of 2400mm (94.5in), the SSM was 3985mm (156.9in) in length, 1695mm (66.7in) wide, and only 1150mm (45.3in) tall. The elegant wedge shape, with traditional long nose and short deck proportions, was given a bonnet that dipped below the raised front wings, with a purposeful snout ahead of it, and enclosed headlight housings that were kept low to match the grille. Small ducts for brake cooling were the only other openings up front, nicely integrated into the lip spoiler. The powerful wheelarches added volume to the design,

Design sketch for the SSM concept car. Other drawings had a TVR Chimaera look about them, while a hint of late Chevrolet Camaro and Porsche Boxster featured in others.

The SSM as it appeared at the 1995 Tokyo Motor Show, with gunmetal grey paintwork (the car was also painted bright red at one point). The headlights are particularly stylish, but would never be able to meet contemporary road car regulations without modification. Pop-up headlights were used on the NSX, but were not considered for the open car due to weight and cost concerns.

The divided Formula One-inspired cockpit of the SSM, with features including a digital read-out for the dashboard, carbon-fibre trim, bucket seats with race harnesses, and a semi-automatic gearbox.

with the clean sides broken only by a vent aft of the front wheel, the steeply angled windscreen, and the roll-over hoops placed behind the seats. A crisp creaseline flowed from the nose all the way around to the tail, which featured a flat bootlid (again, like the bonnet, sitting lower than the wingline), combination lamps that resembled the headlights, a sensible cut-out for the number plate, and a diffuser-type panel surrounding the twin exhaust pipes.

As it happens, thanks to the intervention of Shinya Iwakura, there was another interesting Honda-based roadster on display at the Tokyo Show that year – the 'Argento Vivo' concept car on the Pininfarina stand. This explains the confusion regarding the genesis of the S2000, as many credit the Italian styling house with the design work to this day. This is not true, however, as the S2000 was designed by Honda's own staff, as was the SSM. Notwithstanding, built on a 2500mm (98.4in) wheelbase and some 260mm (10.2in) longer than the SSM, the Argento Vivo was a stunning aluminium and glass-fibre creation, equally luxurious in both looks and trim, with a retractable hardtop, an extruded aluminium spaceframe under the skin, and a 2.5-litre Honda G25A SOHC straight-five for motive power. The notoriously self-indulgent 29th Sultan of Brunei ordered a short run of the car to be built using Mercedes-Benz engines, eventually joining thousands of other vehicles in the Sultan's garage, including around 500 Rolls-Royces!

Meanwhile, the SSM did the rounds on the US and European show circuit, and the rumours started flying. In May 1997, *Automotive News* reported that Pininfarina was going to build the production car for Honda in Italy, which would be based on the Argento Vivo. Well, while Pininfarina may have been involved with Honda on styling

Rear view of the SSM, with the roll-over hoops and diffuser panel surrounding the exhaust pipes dominating.

input from the early 1980s, and the Italian company had a history of building vehicles as well as designing them (indeed, it was about to start producing cars for Mitsubishi at the time), this did seem to be a simple case of putting two and two together and coming up with five. More confusion followed as a result ...

Not long after, in the autumn of 1997, lightly disguised English-registered prototypes were spotted on test, killing off the Argento Vivo rumour straight away, as it was perfectly clear that the production car was going to closely resemble the SSM model, albeit with a convertible top and styling revisions to make the car road legal on the international stage. In time, the source of the design would be made clear, too (not least by the promotional paperwork issued by Honda in 1998), and production would indeed be carried out in Japan.

Questions still remained, of course, particularly concerning the powertrain, with various suggestions of a 1.6 or 2.2-litre VTEC four, a high-revving straight-five,

a small V6, or even an all-alloy 2-litre V5 circulating in the global press. An aluminium body was also mooted to house the unit, with the car picking up the SSX nickname along the way.

NEWS UPDATE
Much to the delight of Honda's long-serving boss in the States, Koichi Amemiya, sales were starting to pick up again in the US. This may have had something to do with the first American-built Acuras going on sale in 1996, or it could have been due to Honda's motorsport success.

Granted, Mercedes-Benz won the 1997 Indy title, but Alex Zanardi secured the drivers' championship, followed home by two other Honda exponents, Gil de Ferran and Jimmy Vasser. Of more importance to European and Asian enthusiasts, perhaps, in spring 1998, Honda announced its intentions to return to the Formula One arena, although at this stage it would be via a joint programme with the UK-based BAR (British American Racing) team.

The Argento Vivo concept car, which made its debut at the 1995 Tokyo Show. Bigger all-round than the SSM, note the wood trim used for the interior.

The Argento Vivo with its retractable hardtop in place to create the equivalent of a closed car. Five replicas were ultimately built, powered by Mercedes-Benz V12s.

There would be a wait, but at least this was a good sign for those who mourned the demise of the last Honda F1 era.

Whilst rumours circulated of a new V8-engined NSX for the new millennium, one thing was for sure: at the end of April 1998, Hiroyuki Yoshino became Honda's fifth President (he was formerly the company's VP).

Yoshino trained as an aeronautical engineer, but ended up in management for much of his career, including heading up the American Honda operation in Ohio. Thankfully, his enthusiasm was every bit as plentiful as that of his predecessors. A string of encouraging results, especially in Indycar racing, would help him keep the faith ...

Two later design sketches, with the S2000 lines clearly showing through by now. The vent on the trailing edge of the front wing was carried over from the SSM, but would be dropped for production cars. Toshiyuki Fukatsu was the main person responsible for transforming Sawai's drawings into scale models.

THE 1998 PROTOTYPE

The 1997 Tokyo Show came and went, but Toyota's MR-S and Suzuki's C2 concept were the only models to prick the interest of traditional sports car fans, with the Toyota going on to become a superb mid-engined plaything soon after. Otherwise, there was a staggering array of awful bubbles and boxes, although the Honda J-VX was a pretty coupé, it has to be said, giving a hint of the Insight to come.

The sense of disappointment was quickly dispelled, however, for on 24 September 1998 – the 50th anniversary of the company – the 'S2000 Prototype' was unveiled to the press at Honda's chic Aoyama offices in downtown Tokyo. There were small details still to be finalised, such as tyre choices and the full equipment listing, but basically, this was, in effect, a carefully staged preview of the production model. With no Tokyo Show for 1998, Honda had the media's full attention, and with full-page adverts in national newspapers to spread the word even further, a case of S2000 fever was as good as guaranteed.

As with the SSM concept model, the production body's lines were the responsibility of Daisuke Sawai. The 1998 car sported a taller windscreen and less aggressive lines, but the dimensions and general shape were admirably similar to those of the SSM. The headlight enclosures retained their striking appearance, but were moved upwards in order to fall into line with the world's road car regulations. This was then balanced with a subtly raised bonnet height, allowing a deeper central intake and heavier-looking 'ducts' below the light units at the same time. It should be noted, however, that the brake vents were dummies on the production car, dressed with a black louvred insert to trick the eye into believing they were operational.

Down the sides, the orifice was dropped on the trailing edge of the front wing, although the character lines in the sill area were still very strong. In addition, more sensible rear-view mirrors and door handles were adopted (both finished in body colour), along with fresh repeater indicators on the front fenders, and a fuel filler on the nearside rear wing. Otherwise, apart from the windscreen profile already mentioned, and the hood stack behind the seats (a power-operated soft top was added to the spec sheet on the showroom model), the lines were remarkably true to those of the 1995 show car. Around the back, too, while a high-mount LED rear brakelight was added to the edge of the bootlid, the only other differences of note were the roll-over hoop shapes and the use of a heavier one-piece bumper moulding, with the SSM's diffuser reduced to a narrow piece of trim sitting above the pair of exhaust pipes.

One area where the SSM and S2000 differed completely, though, was in the cockpit treatment, which naturally had to be toned down – after all was said and done, while the SSM's exterior was fairly realistic in terms of showroom potential, the interior was aimed at wooing the crowds rather than satisfying practical issues and build codes. Gone was the central split, which surprised no-one, and the wraparound driver's pod was replaced by a very traditional dashboard and control layout; the digital dash read-out was the only component that gave a nod to the future, although these things were hardly new, of course. Indeed, they'd been all the rage in the 1980s, and were, if anything, less common at the time of the prototype's launch than they had been when Ronald Reagan was in the White House. Anyway, it was something different, and with cars like the Porsche Boxster, Mercedes-Benz SLK, BMW Z3 and Mazda MX-5 already in the marketplace, there was nothing wrong with trying to create a significant gap in the detailing.

Mechanically, the straight-five engine from the SSM was swapped for an all-alloy straight-four. But carried over from the SSM, the 2-litre capacity chosen for the showroom model was a useful selling point in Japan, as the annual road tax is much cheaper than that for a car breaking the 2000cc threshold. Interestingly, while the NSX had been offered with an automatic (AT) option from the start, and the SSM had hinted at the use of an F-Matic gearbox, the S2000 would only ever be supplied with a manual gearbox, all the way through to its final days.

In keeping with lightweight sports car practice, a double-wishbone suspension was specified, although the rack-and-pinion steering was given electrical assistance rather than a traditional hydraulic setup. The 16in wheel and tyre combination covered disc brakes on all four corners, as one would expect on a vehicle of this type. Five-spoke alloys would be the norm.

THE S2000 IN DETAIL

Having already stated that the 'S2000 Prototype' was basically a production model, bar a few trivial items, we may as well go over the technical side of things here and now, as part of the development story, thus

(Continues page 26)

A WORD FROM THE CHIEF ENGINEER

Born in September 1947, Shigeru Uehara joined Honda in 1971, and, in addition to heading S2000 development, he was the original NSX project chief, too. In other words, combined with his infectious passion and enthusiasm, his credentials for the job of creating a real sports car that delivers "a new level of unity and driving pleasure" - equally at home on a busy street or race track - were impeccable ...

Asked what was the direction wanted for the S2000, Uehara responded: "Most of us wanted to create a new generation of S800 - the distinctive type of machine that brought us into the Honda fold in the first place. Going the classic two-seater FR convertible route seemed logical, as a mid-engined car would have been too similar to the NSX, and President Kawamoto insisted from the start that the S2000 should not be seen as a poor man's NSX - it was to be a thoroughly modern pure sports car that offered its own unique brand of qualities, and would appeal to a wide range of people, including NSX drivers.

"You will be surprised to know that we had very little input from the marketing people. This was a deliberate move, as we wanted to create something to please us

Chief Engineer, Shigeru Uehara, pictured during an interview with the author in January 1999.

Uehara (in the orange shirt) with one of the UK-registered test cars. Following a rubber stamp from President Kawamoto, extensive testing was carried out all over Europe, with rival machines often brought into the equation for comparison.

as an engineering team, rather than try and please everyone. If you listen to everyone, included everything they ask for, all cars end up the same. We wanted a vehicle that was more focused - more Honda.

"The reaction garnered by the SSM meant we had to keep the S2000 as close as possible to the concept car. Using a Civic CRX Del Sol-based mule, it was obvious the packaging was going to be tight, but the early prototype was tried against rival models at Suzuka, and it looked so right, we felt obliged to continue down the same development path.

"As the project evolved, to make sure we were on the right track, we did a lot of real world testing - first in Hokkaido, and then all over Europe, taking in an average of 450 miles (720km) a day at high speed. We wanted a car that delivered just the right amount of tension for the driver, with direct and linear response, sharp handling and the necessary power and torque for fast progress and safe overtaking, but nothing too excessive. The final fine-tuning was done on the track to ensure the handling was right without being that sharp that the car became unruly, whatever the weather, followed by more road testing, including a fair bit around the Hakone area. Ultimately, overall driving feel and sound were considered more important than outright speed."

Testing in progress. These prototypes, the first being spotted on open roads with earlier R (1997) plates, were lighter than production models but had slightly less power. More than 20,000 miles (32,000km) of testing was conducted before the design was signed off.

Interior proposals, with the styling theme being more realistic than it had been on the SSM. Ergonomics played a large part in the design, with switches in logical, easy to reach positions.

strength as cost, although the use of an aluminium bonnet was ultimately given the nod from the beancounters. As such, it's in the details where improvements could be made, rather than revolutionary design work.

Body rigidity is a must to ensure decent handling properties, for a suspension is only as good as the structure to which it is attached. As Honda's people knew all too well from their racing exploits, a shell that twists and bends, even to a small extent, will destroy any accuracy in the suspension setup, so no matter how hard the engineers toil on refining exotic systems, the handling will never be consistent or manage to live up to expectations.

leaving the next chapter free to describe the differences between each market once the car hit the showrooms. For ease of reference, each major component or group of components will be looked at under five separate subheadings.

Body

The styling has pretty much been covered already and, besides, a picture paints a thousand words. But there are a number of aspects regarding the bodywork that need to be recorded for the sake of the book's completeness, with some innovative work aimed at enhancing rigidity and safety whilst keeping weight to a minimum.

In this day and age, monocoque construction can be taken as read on virtually any mass-produced machine. There are still a few cars with a separate ladder frame, such as the Suzuki Jimny off-roader, but generally speaking, a monocoque shell is the norm. The S2000 was no exception to the rule, using steel pretty much throughout – again, the industry norm, as much for

Achieving body strength is difficult enough at the best of times, but with an open car, the task simply becomes that much harder. Roll-over safety is another concern, with the A-posts having to do so much of the work in the creation of a 'safety cell,' and suitable head protection needed aft of the passengers; side impact protection and front and rear crumple zones also have to be factored in, as well as a suitable amount of luggage space. Add in the fact that weight needs to be kept to a minimum for enhanced response, handling and fuel economy, not to mention the existence of some excellent bench mark vehicles already in the arena, and one starts to get an idea of the many challenges facing the body designers.

Having the advantage of being able to start from a clean sheet of paper (rather than try and work on the conversion of a closed car, which is rarely an ideal situation), Honda ultimately came up with what it called the 'High X-Bone Frame,' which incorporated a strong central tunnel that acted like a backbone, high sills (or rocker panels), and diagonal bracing at each side of the cockpit. This hybrid monocoque structure, combined with subframes to look after the suspension mounting at both ends, would ensure a good, flex-free platform on which to build.

There were novel features everywhere one looked, from the U-shaped high-tensile steel front member with two upper lateral braces within to give the bumper mounting added strength (a 40 per cent improvement compared to a traditional square section beam, as it happens) through to doubling up of sleeved pipework in the A-pillar to meet the necessary roll-over requirements. Twin door beams looked after side impact protection, while the layout of the side members distributed load evenly through the doors, sills and floor, and to a slightly greater extent through the central tunnel in the event of a frontal or offset accident. This three-point support structure (where the front sidemember joined the tunnel and sills via angled bracing sections) ensured both enhanced body rigidity and controlled deformation, offering the equivalent level of collision safety as a closed vehicle without any significant weight penalty.

Designed with European tastes and environs in mind, the headlights were an important part of the car's styling, featuring HID xenon projector lights for low beam (regular H1 bulbs were

The Honda S2000 Prototype receiving the attention of a curious press corps. The company used the 'Designed By Honda' phrase to send a strong message and leave little room for doubt regarding who'd created the machine. (Courtesy Miki Press)

The press pack and huge (and therefore all too easily damaged) brochures issued at the launch of the prototype. One is a six page fold-out with three pictures, and the other is one of four showing similar images, plus this extra side view.

Below and opposite: The other two shots used in the oversized brochures issued in September 1998. Although the 'S2000 Prototype' has an extra badge on the tail, production cars would sport only those seen on the front wings and the Honda marque logo at both ends.

employed for high beam) and integrated sidelights, side marker reflectors and indicator units. They gave a distinctive character to the front face, but also played an important role in the car's aerodynamics package.

On the subject of aerodynamics, early research was carried out through computer simulation, speeding along work in the wind tunnel, while the German autobahns were used for confirmation of high-speed stability before the car received a final rubber stamp. The nose shape was designed to cut through the air and reduce lift, while covers in the front wheelarches, joining up with another flat piece below the radiator, helped smooth airflow underneath the car; export models also had spats ahead of the four tyres. Further refinements were made to the door mirror profile, the enclosure for the high-mount rear stoplight, which duly evolved into a tiny spoiler, the lip on the insert above the exhausts, and even the bold rear combination lamp shape. Although a Cd figure was never

published by Honda, independent tests put it at 0.38 with the hood up, and 0.46 in open mode, which seems about right given known values from other makers.

The power-operated soft top was made from a special high-quality black vinyl, which looked and felt like cloth but was easier to care for, with a large clear plastic window in the rear. The latter naturally ruled out the use of heater elements, but the hefty seals worked well at keeping out the weather, and thanks to a special pinion and sector gear setup, after releasing the two clips on the header rail (located near the outer edges of the sunvisors) it took only six seconds to open or close the top at the press of a button. A moulded black hood boot was duly made available as an option in the summer of 1999.

Interior
The design theme was an F1 cockpit, which may sound

silly given the end result, but the key point was not making the interior look like a Formula One machine. Indeed, it was more about creating a focused, driver-first environment – a snug tightness (an impression helped by the high central tunnel and low fascia), excellent ergonomics, with zero offset in the small diameter steering wheel, switchgear and other controls that were precise and easy to use, even with gloves on, and features that would generate excitement, like the digital dash (chosen by Uehara after testing with a McLaren F1 gauge similar to the type used by Ayrton Senna on one of the prototypes), the drilled aluminium pedal set, and the large engine 'start' button, which ultimately began something of a trend within the industry. A glovebox was deliberately left off the spec sheet to enable the stylists to sculpt the fascia as they envisaged it, and even the audio compartment was covered by a lid, lending a more businesslike aura to the T-shaped dashboard and highlighting the simple aluminium gearshift in the process.

Honda's men also knew that for any car to remain enjoyable over a long period, either as a daily driver or a weekend warrior, it had to be comfortable. New, manually adjusted full bucket seats were designed especially for the S2000. There was no height adjustment, but the four-way buckets were supple enough to allow occupants to tour, yet supportive enough for those venturing out onto the track. Although the hip point was slightly higher than that of the NSX, it was still very low, and the driving position was thus very similar to that of its stablemate.

The S2000 was always meant to be an open car, of course, so the interior designers worked hand-in-hand with the body people to nurture a pleasant hood down environment, creating unity with the surroundings. Wind management (both in terms of the amount of air reaching the cockpit and noise) was studied carefully, a point confirmed in such areas as the A-pillar shape through to the netting in the seat headrests, as well as the optional windblocker, placed between the roll-over bars and easy to fold down when not in use. The compact HVAC system was also refined, with the air-conditioning featuring an 'open mode' setting, circulating air lower down to maintain comfort levels, and additional vents high up behind the seats. Further thought on making this a practical car in all weathers can be witnessed in things like the demister vents in the base of the windscreen frame to keep the side glass clear.

As far as the switchgear was concerned, taking a domestic car as a good example of the breed (although it should be noted that apart from the pedals, the locations were reversed on left-hand drive machines, even down to the start button and handbrake), most of the controls were grouped before the driver. Beyond the thick-rimmed leather-clad steering wheel (of three-spoke design, with a centre-push horn, but non-adjustable) was a pair of stalks – wiper and washer controls on the left, indicators and lighting on the right. There was also an ignition switch, using a traditional key, under the indicator wand, to activate the start button and kill the juice feeding the engine, as well as lock/unlock the steering and immobiliser.

Moving on to the main dashboard area, the gauges were arranged in a semi-circular binnacle, with the speedometer in large digital numbers in the centre, and odometer and trip meter figures below in a different colour. The tachometer followed the profile of the upper section of the instrument panel in an arc, rather like a rainbow over the speedo. It used coloured bands to light the meter, all the way up to the 9000rpm red-line. To the left of the rainbow's end was a coolant gauge and dash brightness adjuster, while the fuel gauge and trip function switch was to the right (the latter also had a 'SEL' button alongside it in some markets, allowing the driver to switch from mph to km/h calibrations, and vice versa). A bank of warning lights ran across the lower edge of the pod, with more above the switches in each corner, although main beam and indicator warning lights, with their importance during fast driving duly recognised, were each side of the speed read-out.

There were two zones created either side of the steering column, one via a continuation of the instrument binnacle lines, and a second, almost giving the impression of ears attached to the main moulding, and angled towards the driver, although it was simply a trick of the eye. Anyway, both 'ears' had directional vents in the upper section, while the left-hand bank of switches looked after the heater controls, and that on the right, audio controls and the engine start button. Inside these, were blanking plates on most Japanese cars, although some markets had cruise control switches beyond the indicator wand, with extra buttons on the steering wheel for cars fitted with this gadget.

The dashboard continued across to the passenger side, angled downwards to minimise stray reflections in the windscreen, visually flowing into the door casings, and housing the screen vents, passenger airbag and another air vent close to the door. Some cars had a navigation system, and this was fitted in the same plane as the vent, but closer to the centre of the car when specified. Joining the fascia to the centre tunnel was a short tail to make a 'T' shape, with narrow vents at the top and a lidded compartment for the audio system. Moving back along the tunnel, there was the gearlever, handbrake, hazard warning light and power roof switches, and storage compartments that doubled as a cup holder in one case; more storage was provided in a box between the seatbacks, with upper and lower lids, the latter containing the boot release. Above this bulkhead box, many cars had a folding acrylic windblocker to stop draughts, although it was generally considered an option, while below it was a 12V accessory power socket.

Sunvisors (with a vanity mirror on the passenger side one), roof release catches, interior lights and a mirror sat on the padded header rail, while the doors played host to the stereo speakers and power window lifts, as well as the power door lock and outside mirror adjustment controls on the driver's side. The only other things worth noting were the attractive plaques on the sill covers, the fuel filler release on the driver's door jamb, the bonnet release on the A-post (under the dashboard), the map pockets on the seatbacks, and the storage net in the passenger-side footwell.

Before leaving this section, we should look at safety measures, and the trunk. Dual SRS airbags (situated in the steering wheel boss and upper section of the dashboard on the passenger side) were augmented by three-point ELR seatbelts with pretensioners and load limiters, and ample padding on the doors, windscreen frame, and roll-over hoops. The lined boot (or trunk, depending on which side of the Atlantic you were born) had a deep well in the centre, formed around the exhaust pipes as it happens, with its lid covering a small storage compartment and the car's toolkit. The 50-litre (11 Imperial gallon) fuel tank formed the lower part of the rear bulkhead, with the spacesaver spare on top of it on one side, and a home for the optional CD-changer on the other.

For the record, interior development was led by Yoshinori Asahi, with Koichi Yokomizo looking after the modelling side, and Masayuki Togawa responsible for packaging; Shiho Sawada was in charge of both the interior and exterior colouring, rolling out New Formula Red and Silverstone Metallic paint options especially for the new arrival.

Engine

With the G-series of straight-fives consigned to the history books, and a V6 considered too heavy and bulky after careful deliberation, this left only an inline-four in the arsenal, if one is to be realistic. Honda had plenty of engines to choose from, but rather than lift a unit straight from another machine, the design concept called for something truly exciting – a free-revving four that would deliver exceptional levels of power for a normally-aspirated (NA) engine, and have a red-line more readily associated with racers than showroom models.

The starting point was the F20B, but the all-alloy F20C quickly developed into something quite unique in order to fall in line with the development goals, not only in terms of performance and response but also meeting ever-stricter environmental codes, and in the end, after much trial and error (indeed, people started to lose count of how many engine failures were caused during the quest to achieve the heady 9000rpm limit specified!), the 2-litre VTEC lump ultimately shared hardly any features with the units in its Accord stablemate.

Starting at the bottom and working our way up, the aluminium alloy block was split in two at the crankshaft's horizontal centreline, with a cast main bearing support piece bolted to the upper diecast section that played

Cutaway version of the 2-litre all-alloy 16v VTEC engine chosen to power the S2000.

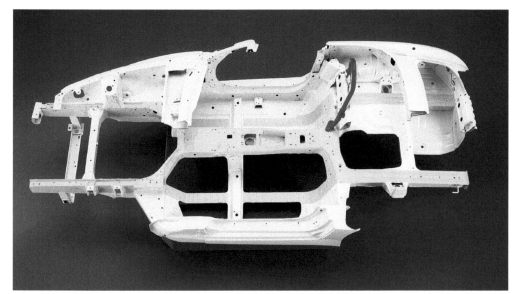

A partially built body prepared for the show circuit, with the 'X-Bone' concept highlighted in yellow. The tall tunnel and sills added the strength one usually lost in the architecture when converting a saloon into a drophead, while the bulkheads, ample cross-bracing and floor panels welded to them tied everything together. Note the roll-over bar behind the cockpit, painted in red and made from 38mm (1.5in) diameter high-tensile steel pipe.

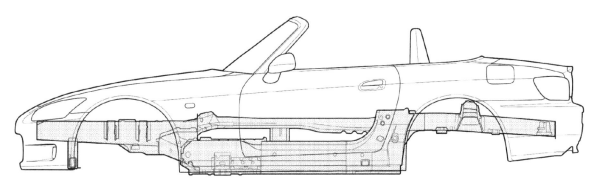

A side view of the 'X-Bone' that formed the basis of the S2000's hybrid monocoque body. Honda's internal test data revealed that torsional rigidity was almost exactly the same as that of a saloon, taking weight into consideration, and far superior to a couple of open bodies either side of the S2000 in terms of bulk. As for bending rigidity, the S2000 shell displayed even better results than the average closed car.

Opposite, top: A different pre-production prototype on view at the Honda offices and showroom at Aoyama. The 'S2000' badge on the tail has already disappeared, giving the car a cleaner, less cluttered look. Prototypes were used for executive transport at the 'Honda 50' event a few days later. (Courtesy Miki Press)

host to corresponding main bearing surfaces and the cylinder bores. The lower ladder frame had cast iron inserts for the mains, ensuring a longer life for the engine, while the main open deck section featured special FRM cylinder liners as an integral part of the casting. FRM, or Fibre Reinforced Metal, is an interesting piece of technology, using carbon fibres embedded in a ceramic material similar to that used in sparkplug insulators. The FRM liners offered excellent heat transfer properties, as well as being hard-wearing and light in weight. More weight was saved via an aluminium alloy sump, which was finned on the leading and lower edges to dissipate heat; a separate compact oil cooler was situated to the offside front of the engine to help further, with the oil filter screwing into the novel water-cooled device.

The forged steel crankshaft ran in five main bearings of the conventional shell type, with an oil channel down the centre. A double toothed sprocket on the nose of the crank allowed one chain to drive the freshly designed high-volume oil pump that sat in the sump, while a second longer one (with an automatic tensioner) ran upwards to a timing sprocket bolted directly to a helical gear that ultimately drove the camshafts. The exotic forged aluminium alloy pistons (a first for a Honda production car) had three rings and short skirts beneath them to reduce friction, and keep weight to a minimum (a must on moving parts if one is to successfully increase engine speeds), while the full-floating pins aided refinement. Connecting rods were slim, heat-treated and carburised steel forgings, with the big-end caps secured by a

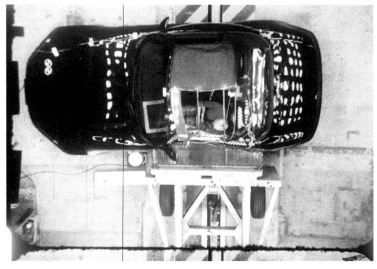

Full frontal, offset and side impact crash testing. The author has actually seen these tests carried out at Honda R&D, and it's a brutal thing to witness. However, the 30mph (50km/h) rear test simply made the car look shorter!

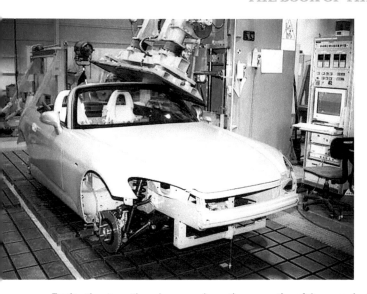

Testing the strength and energy absorption properties of the upper body, first with an applied weight in a controlled fashion, and later in a roll-over situation.

pair of bolts (no nuts), and fitted with regular plain metal shell bearings. The bore and stroke was set at 87.0mm x 84.0mm to give a cubic capacity of 1997cc. It was in the aluminium alloy cylinder head, though, where most of Honda's renowned creativity could be found, as the dohc VTEC variable valve timing system was completely revised for the S2000 application.

A single sparkplug sat in the middle of the domed pent-roof combustion chamber, with a pair of 35mm (1.38in) diameter inlet valves on one side of it, and a pair of 30mm (1.18in) diameter exhaust valves on the other, both angled at a fairly narrow 25.5 degrees off the centre – one of many factors in allowing the F20C unit to be so compact. Based on race experience, a single valve spring was chosen to reduce weight and bulk, with a valve clearance adjusting screw above. This screw was attached to a special rocker arm, made via a new MIM (metal injection moulding) process, which allowed the VTEC system to kick in at 5850rpm by locking the two outer arms to a central one which corresponded to a higher lift profile on both camshafts, giving the valves longer duration and thus letting the engine breathe easier at higher speeds. Honda termed this a roller-type co-axial VTEC rocker arm, as the areas that came into contact with the camshaft lobes (the cam followers, if you like) were actually needle roller bearings, helping reduce frictional losses in the valvetrain by as much as 70 per cent. The three sintered-steel rocker arms pivoted on a hollow steel tube that fed them with oil, held in place by castings that

formed a cradle for the camshafts (themselves hollow, to save weight and simplify lubrication, driven by a compact helical gear for greater accuracy at higher speeds), while the hydraulically operated sliding switch-over pins that allowed the three arms to lock were contained within the roller bores.

The whole VTEC mechanism was dressed with an attractive red rocker cover, with a black centre section that hid the sparkplugs and the direct ignition system, featuring separate high-voltage coils for each cylinder instead of a traditional distributor (the battery was placed to the side of the engine, close to the bulkhead in front of the passenger, by the way). The computer-controlled DI system worked off the data gathered by three main sensors (one on the crankshaft, and one on the tail of each camshaft), plus information on the atmospheric pressure, intake air temperature, throttle opening, knock sensor readings and coolant temperature, which was duly processed by the ECU to determine the spark timing and dwell. Ditching the distributor saved a huge amount of space at the rear of the engine, allowing it to be pushed right back to the bulkhead to give what was almost a front midship layout. This was critical in achieving the 50/50 front-to-rear weight distribution that was listed as a design goal.

The lightweight, alloy intake manifold had an integral large-capacity plenum chamber, and long tuned runners that were almost straight, thus ensuring minimal back pressure and fast response for heel-and-toe fanatics.

The clear lens headlight unit chosen for the S2000, seen here in US-spec guise. Note the simple grille in the air intake, and the brake ducts, which were actually a sham with dressing pieces to make them look real. The impact-absorbing bumpers naturally passed the 5mph (8km/h) knock test with ease, and were colour-keyed to match the rest of the bodywork.

Honda's multi-point programmed fuel-injection (PGM-FI) was employed, an electronically-controlled sequential system, with the injectors tucked up tight to the cylinder head and covered by a black dressing piece to give the installation a neat appearance. Incidentally, thanks to the rearward bias of the engine, the air cleaner setup could be placed well ahead of the engine, thus keeping incoming air as cool as possible, as well as allowing stylists to retain a low bonnet height.

As for the exhaust, the lengthy 4-2-1 manifold-cum-downpipe was fabricated from stainless steel tubing to save weight (exhaust headers are traditionally made from cast iron) and provide the most efficient gasflow possible. The single pipe then attached to the catalytic converter before travelling back to a small central muffler, whereupon it branched out into a pair of back boxes via a Y-piece. Incidentally, the back boxes had a U-turn pipe within them to reduce back pressure, and big bore tailpipes to provide a throaty sound. Emissions were looked after by the aforementioned high-efficiency metallic honeycomb catalytic converter, with oxygen sensors fore and aft, and an electronic air pump controlling the multi-port air-injection system. Between them (combined with the engine's high c/r, promoting a cleaner burn), the S2000 was able to boast some quite remarkable reductions in CO, HC and NOx levels, easily passing all known worldwide emission codes at the time.

The engine was water-cooled, of course, with the radiator and electric fan in the nose of the car, just beyond the main air intake, and the water pump driven by a single ribbed belt that also drove the alternator, and air-conditioning compressor. In another shining example of Honda's fetish with saving space and weight reduction, the water pump housing contained the thermostat, and also moved sideways enabling it to act as a lower bracket for the alternator. Ultimately, the dressed F20C unit ended up at around the same size as a 1.6-litre Civic powerplant.

With a high compression ratio of 11.7:1, the domestic 2-litre engine gave 250PS on 98-octane fuel, along with 160lbft of torque. The linear power curve didn't tail off until the red-line, while the torque curves remained beefy, and almost flat, as the VTEC system kicked in to save the day. Thanks to VTEC, Honda's specific output figures have always been interesting, with the early Preludes delivering around 100PS per litre (once the realm of pure racing engines), rising to 110PS with the 1996 Integra Type-R, but the S2000's 125PS per litre was remarkable, and easily a world-leading number to reckon with. At the same time, developed under Toru Karaki in the main, it was a clean unit, qualifying the new car for LEV status due to its low emissions.

An early prototype in the wind tunnel.

The US-spec S2000 with its hood up – a pre-production car, as it happens, as the badging is wrong for a US model (see next chapter for details). The lightweight top and its linkage tipped the scales at around 27kg (60lb). By the way, there were no thoughts of producing a coupé version of the car, but a removable hardtop was already waiting in the wings.

The interior of a JDM S2000 at the time of its domestic launch. Outward visibility, simplicity, comfort and control feel were design priorities, aimed at creating what Honda called an "interfusion" between car and driver.

Transmission

Honda's engineers devised an all-new six-speed manual transmission for the S2000. Mounted in the same plane as the engine, as with the entire drivetrain, it was designed to be as light, compact and rigid as possible, aiding vehicle response, and thus enhancing driver enjoyment.

All gears, including reverse, were placed on two parallel shafts, coupled at the output end via what Honda termed an independent output reduction (IOR) geartrain – a feature borrowed from the company's FF machines, reducing the number of cogs involved, which in turn reduced the load on the gear synchronisers by as much as 40 per cent, thereby reducing shift effort. Gearchange effort was further reduced by the use of double-cone synchros on first, third and fourth, and employing a newly-developed triple-cone synchroniser on second. Transmission noise was

"Gentlemen, start your engines!" A early Japanese advert highlighting the novel start button arrangement, with an inhibitor on the clutch.

reduced during development, as the characteristic note coming from the gears, whilst interesting at first, was found to become tiresome with the passage of time!

The shift linkage was mounted on top of the three-piece alloy transmission casing – a hefty, well-supported steel bar that eliminated any play between the selector forks and the ball at the base of the hollow gearlever. Hard plastics were used for bearing surfaces in the gearlever in a further bid to provide the driver with a good level of communication. Indeed, with such

extremely short shift strokes specified for the SCYM-type gearbox, a direct feeling was a must. NVH was cut through careful analysis of data, revealing the perfect gearbox mount positions to eliminate primary vibrations.

As can be seen on the markings atop the aluminium alloy gearknob, the forward gears were selected through a traditional double-H pattern gate, with first up and to the left, and sixth down and to the right; reverse was to the right of sixth in a fourth plane, the gearlever having to be pushed down first to overcome the lockout

(Continues page 43)

The HVAC (heating, ventilation and air-conditioning) system was well thought through, allowing occupants to stay as comfortable with the hood down as with it in the closed position.

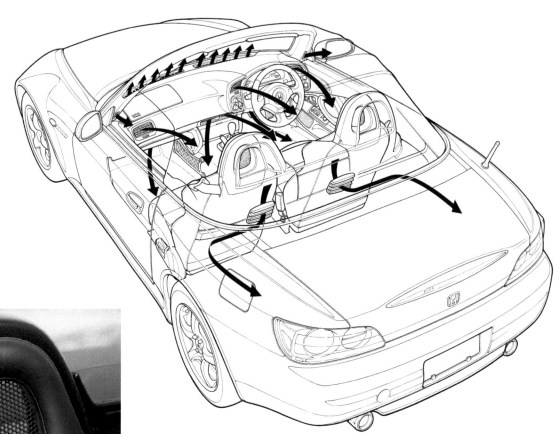

The net used to control airflow in the seat's fixed head restraint (the seats came with fore/aft and backrest angle adjustment only). To the right, one can also see the windblocker – generally an option, and seen here erected. It could be folded down when not in use.

Taking off the door affords a better view of the interior. Although there was no glovebox, several useful storage compartments could be found everywhere. Note the map net on the transmission tunnel, and the elegant plaque on the sill trim.

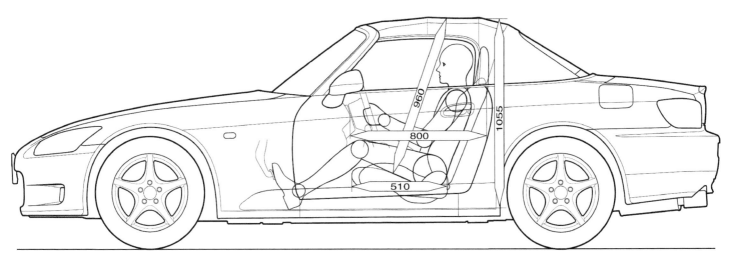

Ergonomics played a major role in the creation of the cockpit. Despite the deliberately tight atmosphere, there was plenty of room for drivers of all builds. Luggage space was quoted as being 152 litres (5.4 cubic feet), which is very reasonable for a car of this type.

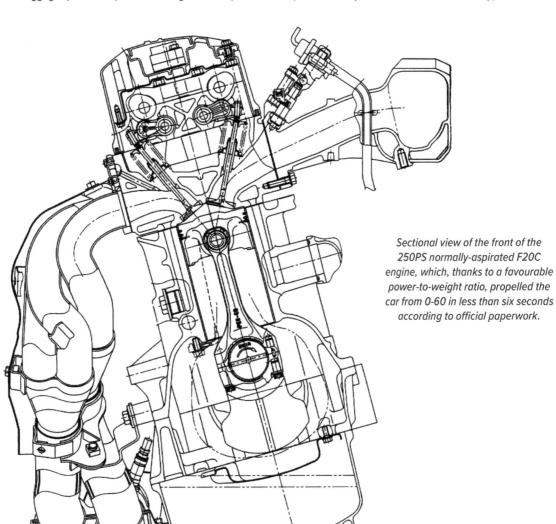

Sectional view of the front of the 250PS normally-aspirated F20C engine, which, thanks to a favourable power-to-weight ratio, propelled the car from 0-60 in less than six seconds according to official paperwork.

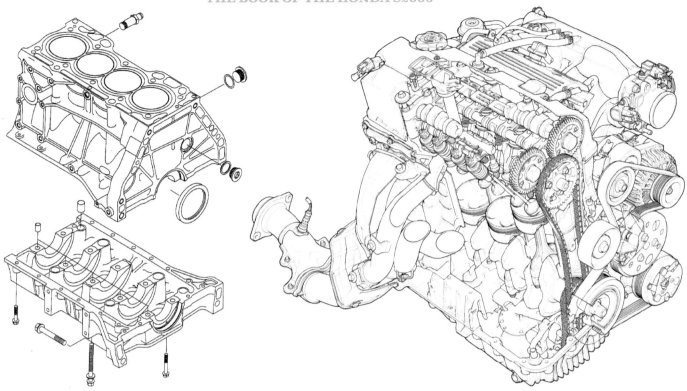

The two-part block used for the 2-litre unit.

Cutaway drawing of the S2000 powerplant viewed from the front. The exhaust system can clearly be seen on the left, with the intake setup to the right, above the alternator.

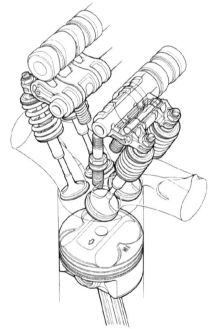

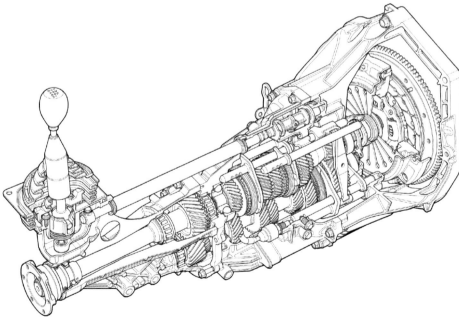

The twin-cam VTEC mechanism in detail. The VTEC variable valve timing system was there to optimise torque delivery over a wide rev range, improving both drivability at lower engine speeds and top-end performance.

The SCYM-type six-speed manual transmission (often abbreviated to 6MT) and clutch setup. The key component in the IOR mechanism is the shaft immediately below the gearshift with taper-roller bearings on it.

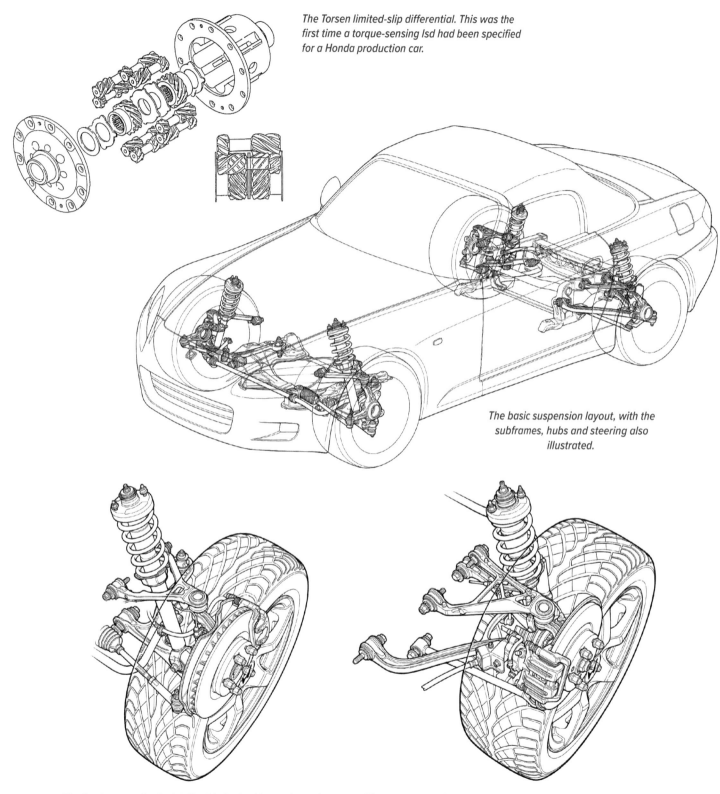

The Torsen limited-slip differential. This was the first time a torque-sensing lsd had been specified for a Honda production car.

The basic suspension layout, with the subframes, hubs and steering also illustrated.

The front suspension in detail, with the braking and steering systems also included.

The rear suspension and brakes. A mechanical handbrake mechanism was built in to work on the rear discs.

Left: The standard alloy wheels for the US market, this being a front one, which was a fraction narrower than those used at the back. While the sizes were the same, the design was slightly different to the ROW wheel, with the spokes sitting inside the rim.

Below: The alloys used for Japan, Europe (including the UK) and Australia. Enkei made the rims, while Bridgestone developed the tyres exclusively for the S2000. Note the headlight washer on this European-spec model.

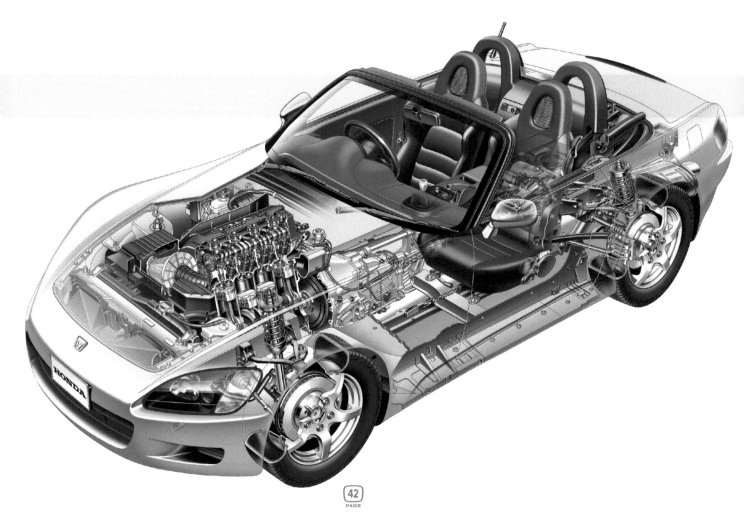

mechanism. The close-ratio gearing was selected to give linear progress and get the most out of the engine's torque curve, with internal ratios of 3.13 on first, 2.04 on second, 1.48 on third, 1.16 on fourth, 0.97 on fifth, and 0.81 on sixth.

Honda's race experience could be seen in areas like the separate oil pump for the transmission, ensuring positive lubrication regardless of the G-loading on the car, and the lightweight flywheel, said to be 20 per cent lighter than that of the contemporary Accord. Ultimately, the loss of weight (or mass) in rotational parts, reduces inertia, which in turn cuts the reaction time between driver input and vehicle response. The hydraulically-operated single dry plate clutch was also designed with this in mind, being as compact as possible, having a pull-type pressure plate, but featuring double-layer friction material on the drive plate for added strength.

The S2000 had a front engine, rear-wheel drive (FR) layout, of course – something of a rarity for recent production Hondas, which have tended to employ an FF configuration for decades. A short, one-piece propshaft

The S2000 flyer produced for the Los Angeles Show, which opened to the public on 2 January 1999. As the paperwork states, the car was due to filter through to American dealers in the autumn of that year, to be sold as a 2000 model.

was employed to take drive from the gearbox to the 4.10:1 back axle, with sliding CV joints at each end to reduce NVH and transmit power more evenly than a traditional universal joint setup. A hypoid-bevel Torsen limited-slip differential was selected for the back-end, which automatically fed torque to the wheel with the most traction, thereby limiting wheelspin and ensuring a continuous flow of power to the driven wheels. To

Cover of the February 1999 issue of Japan's Car Graphic.

make sure none of the engineering effort was wasted, power was taken from the lsd to the rear wheels via exceptionally rigid one-piece driveshafts, bolted directly to flanges at the differential end to ensure a true response to throttle input.

Suspension and other chassis items

Chassis development was led by Ryoji Tsukamoto, whose job it was to make the most of the car's 50/50 weight distribution and low centre of gravity by devising a lightweight suspension that would combine excellent handling on a winding road with a ride quality that made the S2000 equally capable of being used on the track or for the daily commute. Tsukamoto was blessed with an ideal starting point, of course, having a strong bodyshell to work with, and so much of the vehicle's mass placed between the axles, thus reducing the yaw moment of inertia, which translated into a quicker, more linear steering response. The wide wheelarches also allowed him to adopt a wide track in relation to the body length,

enhancing roadholding and stability by default.

An all-round double-wishbone suspension sprang easily to mind, but that adopted on the S2000 was not like a familiar conventional setup of yore. Indeed, mounted on strong fabricated steel subframes, the unequal-length in-wheel system (Honda jargon to promote the impression of compact dimensions) used a different design at each end to endow the suspension with a high level of rigidity, a low unsprung weight, despite the use of ductile steel for all the links (costs had to be taken into account), and an optimum geometry to provide neutral handling, the desired amount of steering feel, and excellent anti-squat properties.

The front suspension consisted of a traditional upper A-arm that had the angled spring-and-damper unit running through its centre, with the coil spring at the top. The tubular shock absorber (the refinement and efficiency in controlling weight transfer and roll afforded by the gas-filled shocks played a crucial role in providing the S2000 with its all-round ability) was secured to the suspension tower at the body side, and the L-shaped arm (a wide-span modified wishbone, in effect, to avoid toe angle changes in cornering) at the lower end, which was then bolted to the hub carrier and subframe in three locations. The setup was completed by a ball-jointed 28.2mm (1.11in) diameter anti-roll bar that ran ahead of the steering rack.

At the back, the upper A-arm sat ahead of the spring-and-damper unit, with the latter being interesting inasmuch as it had a separate gas chamber to overcome packaging problems. As with the front-end, the strut was secured to the body's suspension tower at the top, and the wishbone arrangement at the bottom, which in this case consisted of a wide arm attached to the trailing edge of the hub carrier, a toe control arm running underneath it (fixed to the leading edge of the hub carrier at one end and the subframe at the other), and a 27.2mm (1.07in) anti-roll bar located at the back of the vehicle.

Steering was via a rack-and-pinion system with electrical power assistance (EPS), which was fast to react, light and compact, and saved around 5bhp of power drain compared to a conventional hydraulic PAS system. Similar to that used on the NSX, the rack had an electric motor attached to it, controlled by a microprocessor that varied the amount of assistance given according to vehicle speed, from parking manoeuvres warranting full boost, down to none at all at the top end of the performance spectrum. With the steering ratio set to give a quick 2.4 turns lock-to-lock, the kingpin and caster angles were also optimised to enhance steering feel.

The ABS braking system consisted of discs on all four corners – 300mm (11.8in) in diameter and ventilated up front, and solid 282mm (11.1in) items at the rear. The unusual single-pot calipers specified all-round were designed especially for the S2000, with larger pistons and pad areas employed at the front, in keeping with the car's weight transfer under braking. In the interests of weight distribution, the cast iron calipers were placed on the trailing edge of the discs at the front of the car, and the leading edge at the rear, thus keeping as much bulk as possible between the axles. The servo and master cylinder were tuned to give good feedback through the pedal, despite the anti-lock braking system, which usually takes away a certain amount of feel. With regard to the ABS, this was a compact Honda-designed

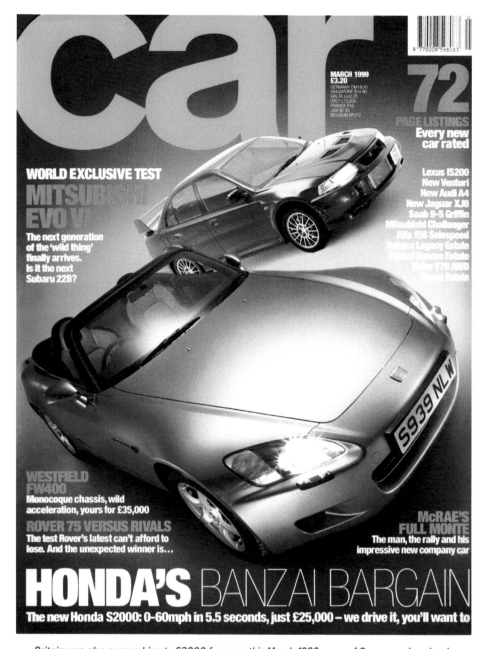

Britain was also succumbing to S2000 fever, as this March 1999 cover of Car magazine clearly illustrates.

system with a speed sensor placed at each wheel, and an ECU controlling the two front slave cylinders independently and the rear ones as a pair to give a three-channel setup.

The S2000 was shod with specially-developed tyres, with wider rubber specified for the rear (225/50s versus the 205/55s used up front). These Bridgestone Potenza S-02s came with a V-shaped tread pattern to disperse

water efficiently, whilst the compound was selected for hard use on tarmac. Interestingly, they were VR-rated in Japan, but WR elsewhere, although the use of 6.5J (front) and 7.5J (rear) rims as their host was universal. The regular alloys were five-spoke wheels, with BBS six-spoke rims (the same sizes, and also produced from aluminium alloy, but 2kg/4.5lb a rim lighter) offered as an option in most markets.

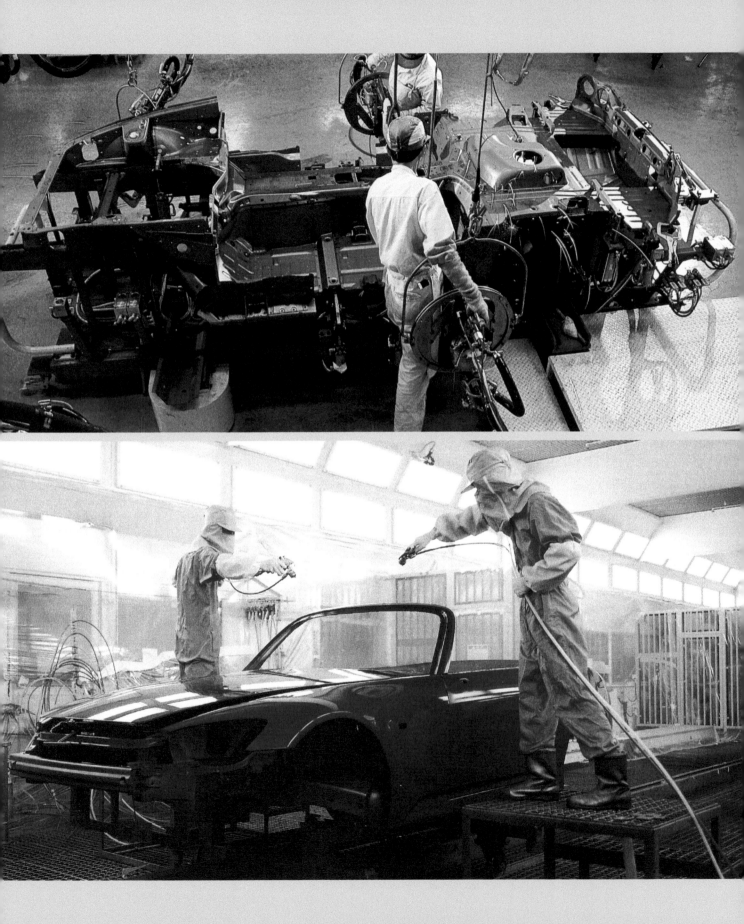

Opposite: S2000 production at the Takanezawa Plant. It starts with the building up of the shell, and completed via a combination of spot welds and hand welding, which is then duly painted and trimmed. The car goes down the line, still in the same building, gaining its powertrain and so on whilst being put together by Honda's more elite workers in a total of 161 operations, before a final water leakage and quality control check.

ALMOST THERE ...

Following the domestic debut of the prototype in the autumn of 1998, the new Honda was duly displayed in all corners of the globe. Honda's new boss, Hiroyuki Yoshino, said of the newcomer: "In line with today's focus on safety and environment preservation, the S2000 is the latest addition to Honda's line of sports cars designed for pure driving pleasure, and shows the direction in which Honda car design is headed for in the future."

In parallel, a number of journalists were invited to try pre-production vehicles in Japan. Writing for *Car* in the UK, Paul Horrell noted: "Moving away, warming up, the S2000 runs like a Civic ... But stretch it, using all six gears to keep it doing its stuff (assume that 6000rpm is where you change down, not up), and then the engine is scintillating, grasping higher and higher crank speeds like some sort of crazed heavy metal guitarist grinding his fingers all the way up the fretboard. Except you'll like the sound. The car doesn't seem to want a higher gear and neither will you.

"This car is all about the art of the possible, and more particularly about Honda's ability to prove that what's impossible for everyone else is possible for Honda. At a price that the opposition would probably find equally impossible: This is faster than a [Porsche] Boxster and £10,000 cheaper. And if you believe, as many do, that Honda is the maker of the world's best engines, and that the engine is in turn the heart of any sports car, then we're looking at something that moves the game on."

JGTC exponent, Takayuki Kinoshita, was also impressed with the engine and drivetrain, but warned the car would not suit everyone. As the likes of *Best Motoring*'s Motoharu Kurosawa had proved flat out at the Nürburgring, driven hard, it was easy to enjoy the S2000's performance, but was likely to bite the inexperienced or unwary. It was a focused machine, and

should be regarded as such. Indeed, the author felt much the same after his first run in the model on a skidpan, although the handling limits were so high that few regular users would ever approach, let alone encounter, that 'knife edge' that kicked in all of a sudden as the physics overtook the engineering, especially on regular roads.

Confirming this observation, *Car & Driver*'s Larry Webster stated: "The chassis tuning is nearly perfect, and the tyres always feel precisely planted. The car communicates a clear picture of what's happening at the contact patch, and as in most Hondas, we could use every last ounce of the 0.90g of lateral grip with complete confidence. The S2000 takes a definite set in corners, but it never feels stuck in one position. It's always ready to change direction yet tracks arrow straight when asked.

"The ride is firm but not harsh, [while] the brakes only enhance the S2000's confidence-inspiring nature. They're strong. Even better, the brake feels firm, and the car doesn't do a nosedive when braking hard.

"As icing on the cake, Honda eliminated some traditional sports car vices. There's plenty of legroom, even for six-footers. There's a dead pedal for your left foot, and enough room in the pedal box to allow unhampered footwork. The power soft top lowers in six seconds ... Storage space is at a minimum. But who cares? You want storage space, get a Honda Odyssey."

Motor Trend added: "It's one of the most solid drop-tops we've driven. Absent is the dash shake of most convertibles. With the top down, there's minimal wind noise and buffeting, especially with the optional windblocker in place." In a different article from the same magazine, the writer finished it with the words: "Thanks, Honda, for giving us such a swell present on your birthday."

During this time, it was announced that the S2000 would be produced at the purpose-built two-storey facility known as the Takanezawa Plant (part of Honda's sprawling Tochigi Factory, which dated back to 1970), situated about 50 miles/80km north of Tokyo. This had officially opened on 30 August 1990, although, in reality, several NSXs had already been built there by then. The S2000 line became operational on 10 March 1999, with the production of 15,000 cars planned for the 2000 season ...

Debut of
the production model

Long launches were becoming the industry norm in the fashionable convertible segment by this time – a teaser, in the shape of a quasi-realistic concept, then a 'close to production' model, with extensive press previews, and then the real thing, often released in different markets in a staggered fashion to ensure yet more coverage in the media. It was no different with the new Honda. At last, though, after a seemingly endless build-up, people were able to buy an S2000 ...

Although Americans and Europeans had already seen the S2000 in the flesh by the spring of 1999, they would have to wait just a little longer before it was made available in the showrooms, for Honda made the decision to release the car in the home (JDM) market first. In fact, domestic orders started being taken soon after the 'S2000 Prototype' debut, despite final specs and pricing still having to be arranged. Given this situation, yes, the 'economic

The S2000 with BBS alloys, as seen in the Japanese press release from the spring of 1999, with the car at last ready to hit the showrooms. Incidentally the first cars were given the AP1-100 internal designation.

Two adverts from April 1999 magazines, with the artwork duplicated in the first domestic catalogue. Over the next few months, going into the New Year, the Japanese media was bombarded with promotional material, with many of the catalogue illustrations used alongside a page of writing to describe a salient feature, such as the engine, aerodynamics, safety, and so on.

bubble' may have burst at the beginning of the 1990s, but one wouldn't have known it. Indeed, there was a backlog of 6000 orders in the first month, which isn't bad considering the company was intending to make 15,000 cars in total for the extended 2000 season!

Officially, Japanese sales started on 15 April 1999, with deliveries scheduled for the summer, and 500 cars a month being the expected volume. The S2000 was sold through the Verno sales channel, mainly for sporting machinery, including the NSX. For the record, the other Honda channels at this time were the Primo one for family cars, and the Clio dealerships for the classier lines.

Priced at 3,380,000 yen, the S2000 came fully loaded, with five-spoke alloy wheels, a limited-slip differential, HID lights, a power soft top, power mirrors,

power windows with UV-cut glass, remote control keyless entry (separate doors and bootlid control), manual air-conditioning, power-assisted steering with a leather-wrapped steering wheel, sports pedals, an aluminium gearknob, a radio/cassette with two speakers, an integrated engine immobiliser, lockable oddment boxes, a 12V accessory socket, warning buzzers for those forgetting to turn off the headlights or leaving the key in the ignition, and a maplight.

Maker options included 16in BBS alloys at 200,000 yen a set, leather seats at 100,000 yen, a DVD-based navigation system at 220,000 yen, and a speed warning buzzer. Dealer options included the folding windblocker (20,000 yen), a soft top boot (55,000 yen), a titanium gearknob (15,000 yen), driver's kneepads (30,000 yen), floormats (35,000 yen, in red or black), a seatback net (4000 yen), and uprated brake pads (40,000 yen). For the more adventurous, there was a Mugen MF10 17in alloy wheel option, with wider 7.5J front and 8.5J rim widths, and priced at 264,000 yen a set. There was also a front lip spoiler at 50,000 yen, complete with the rubber gaiters used on ROW cars, a piece set before the rear wheels with rubber underbody appendages at 38,000 yen, and a bootlid spoiler, listed at 50,000 yen.

Other accessories included a number plate frame (3000 yen), a dedicated full car cover (20,000 yen, or less for the upper body only version), locking wheelnuts, all-weather tyres, snowchains, a child booster seat, an air-conditioning filter, and numerous audio upgrades, including a radio/CD player, a radio/MD player, a CD or MD changer and better speakers, plus traffic situation (VICS) receivers, a cheaper navi system and a TV tuner – an option specified by virtually all Japanese buyers nowadays, and one that the author has never quite been able to understand.

Car Graphic gave the new car a full test in its July 1999 edition. Even though he frowned upon certain details, like the digital dash, having clocked a 0-60 time of 6.3 seconds, Koki Takahira was seriously impressed by the body rigidity, along with the engine's eco credentials, gearshift quality and brakes. Interestingly, he also noted that the suspension tuning was slightly softer than it had been in the prototypes, which makes sense given the state of Japanese roads and the generally slower traffic. In the conclusion, however, while there was an awful lot to applaud, the writer came away feeling there was something missing in the details. He found himself looking forward to the car maturing, in much the same way as the NSX had.

The same magazine put the S2000 up against the Porsche Boxster, and the price difference (3,680,000 yen for the Honda, as tested, against 6,780,000 yen for the German car) naturally made a gap appear in the level of fixtures and fittings. But what was fascinating was the lack of common ground in so many other areas – the kinder Porsche came out ahead in many, except body rigidity and fuel consumption, but personal tastes mean there's more to life than test figures, of course. Those that love VTEC-powered Honda products would doubtless plump for the S2000, while fans of Teutonic machinery would vote in favour of the Stuttgart thoroughbred. Horses for courses as they say ...

The 250PS S2000's appeal was further extended in February 2000 via the availability of a lined aluminium hardtop, which weighed only 20kg (44lb), and came with a heated glass rear window. Listed in all six body colours from the off (hues of black, red, white, silver, blue and yellow), it employed the original locks on the screen header rail, and two new ones at the rear. Buyers could also specify a useful folding stand with casters and a dedicated cover.

(Continues page 57)

JAPANESE (JDM) EARLY AP1 COLOUR AND TRIM OPTIONS

This sidebar charts the changes in the coachwork colour and interior trim for the JDM S2000, the date being the month in which sales of updated vehicles began.

September 1999: Silverstone Metallic, Berlina Black, New Formula Red, Monte Carlo Blue Pearl, Indy Yellow Pearl, and Grand Prix White coachwork colours. Trim came in black vinyl with a cloth insert, with black leather as an option; red leather was available with the silver, black or white paint shades. Hood available in black only.

July 2000: Midnight Pearl paintwork added. All cars now available with red leather trim as an option.

September 2001: Colour palette revised to include Silverstone Metallic, Sebring Silver Metallic, Berlina Black, Midnight Pearl, New Formula Red, Monte Carlo Blue Pearl, Nürburgring Blue Metallic, Indy Yellow Pearl and Grand Prix White as regular paint shades, with Platinum White Pearl, Monza Red Pearl, Lime Green Metallic and New Imola Orange Pearl offered as additional 'Premium' choices. Trim came in black vinyl with a cloth insert, with black, red, red/black or blue leather as an option. Hood now available in black or blue.

October 2002: Midnight Pearl paintwork dropped. Special limited edition 'Gioire' model added with Royal Navy Blue Pearl and Dark Cardinal Red Pearl paintwork, plus tan leather trim.

クルマを愛する君しして

趣味を走る君として。

Selected pages from the first
Japanese brochure.
(Pages 51-55)

スポーツカーの魅力の源泉、それは、身体機能の感覚装置という、クルマの本質にいったもまっ直ぐであることだ。だからこそ、スポーツカーは人間にいちばん近いクルマでなければならない存在なのだ。人と対峙する存在だ。人の意志を、機敏なニュアンスにいたるまで忠実に実行する。そんな一体感に満ちたスポーツカーを操り、思いどおりの走りを実行したとき、ドライバーは無限大の歓びを感じるのです。

物理法則を味方に付けるスポーツカーパッケージング

人馬一体感とは、スキを使ったり、人はわな手綱うちも込なく、思いどおりの道筋を、思いどおりの速度で進んでくれる
人と馬の関係から生まれた言葉です。そんな感覚を、私たちは人とクルマの関係に求めました。馬のような意志がないかわりに、
クルマの動きは物理法則というには見えない力を物を配する力に動いています。
最初に取り組んだのは、この「見えるべき神の下でもいうべき物理法則を味方に付けるスポーツカーパッケージングの追求でした。
軽量・コンパクト理想的な車重均分配と低い燃費イモーメントといった、運動体としての優れた基本特性こそが、
人とクルマの一体感を極めるための大前提になると考えたからです。

まず、スタートポイントとして、フロントエンジン・リアドライブ（FR）の採用を決断しました。
FRとは、ドライバーがスキを存在のスキに応じて、クルマをコントロールする整いやすいという特機を実現でいます。
そんなFRレイアウトの特機を最大限に活かすために、エンジンの小型軽量化、低重心点の質の化を徹底的に追求。
エンジンをフロントアクスルの後方に搭載するFRミッドシップレイアウトを実現。加えて、バッテリー、
スペアタイヤ、燃料タンクといった重量部物を中心に集め、50:50という理想的な前後車重均分を達成すると共に、
ヨーイング中に慣性モーメントをできるだけ低性能モーメントが小さくしています。

パッケージングに加え、車重化基本性能になるのが車体剛性です。サスペンションを設計通りに動くに、
それに見合うボディが、路面からの振動や、コーナリング、ブレーキングで生じる力に耐える「かたさ」が求められます。
しかもS2000は、一般的にボディ剛性を高めにくいとされるオープンボディを採用しているため、十分なボディ剛性の確保は命題でした。
そこで私たちは、オープンカーのボディ剛性を飛躍的に高める独自の技術を開発して、通車各2本のサイドバーを、
通常より高い位置に配したフロントトンネルを持った「X」型に交し、「ハイXポーンフレーム構造」です。S2000では、
この前後フレームに大断面サイドメンバーを組み合わせることで、クローズドボディにも匹敵するボディ剛性を確保しました。

●ハイXポーンフレーム構造
機体剛性の中をしっかりと確保するため
にしたX型を使ったスポーツカー独自の
ボディ構造。車体前後のメンバーをX型
で交したハイXボーンフレーム構造と、
大断面のフロントトンネル、前後2本の
大きなサイドメンバーを特化する事で、高
い車体剛性を実現。これまでクローズド
ボディにもなる高いボディ剛性を確保。
オープンボディなのに軽量化との両立が
性を高いなに実現している。

右足の繊細な動きに即応するレスポンス、心地いい振動、回転数によって表情を変える軽快なサウンド、わき上がるパワー
S2000専用の直列4気筒DOHC VTECエンジンは、高度な環境性能を満たしながら、内燃機関ならではの素晴らしい
エンターテイメント性で、人とクルマの一体感を究極まで高めます。

これからのスポーツカーに相応しいパワーユニットを目指して

さらなる高出力と、クリーン化を目指して、市販用ガソリンエンジンとして異例の11.7という高圧縮比を、S2000のために
新たに設計したVTECエンジンを組み合わせ、その結果、平成12年排出ガス規制の基準値を大幅に下回る環境対応度を実現しながら、
リッター91.9,000rpm、最高出力250ps・8,300rpm（ネット値）を達成。直列4気筒DOHC VTECエンジンは、これまでの高性能エンジンの
頂点となる最後高のパワーユニットです。

最高出力の追求とともに私たちが本腰したのは、そこにいたるまでの「過程」です「右のアクセル」は、一般的な大きさの
性能曲線輪郭の全域・全否容容のエンジンの鳴き加え、さきまさまなスロット環境におけるエンジン特性を
コスメにイメージ化したものです。特機的な全ポイントは、すべての領域において、ドライブフィールをスポイルするような片りの谷が
発生していないこと。これは、ピーターパワーの追求だけじゃ、スロット環境の大きな過度な目動の特性に動きをかけていた成果です
全開時の胸がするような加速感をもちろん、クルージング状態からスムスと段々に入っていった時、にもっと敏感に
応えてくれるエンジンレスポンスは、ドライバーとクルマの一体感を大きく向上させます。

また、エンジンの小型化を小形化やメカニカル消み込み鳴みの低減化にも注ぎました。カムシャフトチェーン駆動化によるバワーチェーン
機機駆動システムによって歯車地を短縮きるなど、小型軽量化を機械的に追求した結果、従来のわが社のDOHC VTECエンジンに対し、
長さ、幅に大幅な低減に成功。エンジンの小型軽量化は、運動性能向上に大きく貢献しています。

●カムチェーン駆動システム
従来のオイルレベルな化に代え、静機機性に優
れた新開発サレント・チェーンを採用。バルブ
システムは軽量コンパクトをポイントにしたそ
れぞれの駆動を低サイズ化するなど、動きの少
な機構を実現。さらに、カムチェーン系の
ノイズをカット、より快音・高付けば、カム
ノイズチェーン・システムへ一層の軽量化を
アップリフトうえ成機機化を動くにして。機機
駆動システムの軽量化も有機化を実現させてて
いる。

気持ちよさを極めるパワーテクノロジー

一方、どこまでも伸びる爽快な加速フィール実現のため、ローラー同軸VTEC構造をキーテクノロジーとし、さらにホンダ四輪市販車初のアルミ鍛造ピストンや鍛造コンロッドといった様々な高回転化対応技術を投入、9,000rpmという、市販最高レベルの最高回転数を達成しました。換気系には、4-2-1のステンレスパイプ製と1体エキゾーストマニホールドおよび高効率デフィンセンサーを採用。低背圧による大幅なパワーアップと共に、スポーツカーらしい刺激的なエンジンサウンドと低騒音を両立しています。クラッチは、回転慣性の高い小型部材に軽鉄材を振り付けた短構造タイプにすることで高回転化に対応。同時に、フライホイールの慣性質量を2.ivクラス最小レベルとして、アクセル操作に鋭敏に反応する機敏なレスポンスを実現しています。

また、デフマウントシャフトには、駆動力を無駄なく伝達、かつコーナーでのコントロール性を高めるセントLSD（リミテッドスリップデフ）を採用しています。

エンジンとタイヤの間にあって、パワーを伝達するという意味で、駆動系の剛性は、加速時のダイレクト感に大きな影響を与えます。S2000は、1ピースプロペラシャフト、大体なドライブシャフト、さらにワイドスパンに配置したデフマウントにより、「引足と機材が直結している」かのような、ダイレクトな加速レスポンスを実現しました。

トランスミッションには、高回転、高出力型エンジンの能力を余すところなく引き出す、ダイレクトチェンジ形式の新開発6速マニュアルトランスミッションを採用しました。ギヤ比は、9,000rpmでシフトアップした後、高速バイパイオインでの高いトルクバンドで連続的につながっていくクロスレシオに設定。IOR（Independent Output Reduction gear train 独立出力機構）やトリプルコーンシンクロ（2速）&ダブルコーンシンクロ（1、3、4速）などをもちながら、手首の動きだけで小気味よく決まるシフトチェンジとあいまって、とぎれのない刺激的な加速感と、走行シーンにあった最適な駆動力をコントロールして走る醍醐味を満喫できます。

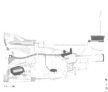

■新設計DOHC VTEC
ホンダの四輪車初採用のアルミ鍛造ピストンの採用により軽量化をめざめのパッケージを実現し軽量化。また、ローラー内蔵式VTEC機構を採用することにより新設計DOHC VTEC機構としている。

■アルミ鍛造ピストン&鍛造コンロッド
対策は自動車のアルミ鍛造ピストンの採用により、ピストンの軽量化をめざめ、コンロッドに新設計軽量化機構を実現した。コンロッドのパワーアップを実現した、二速成のみの選。

■新設計マニュアルトランスミッション
シフトレバー（6速ミッション）ショートケーブルさせるダイレクトチェンジ形式を採用した機構。

Photo : ボディカラー（上）&（ハーパリックオレンジ 左車ーリ、消GLフトっ&ノーネテリオブット、ソフトトップ（ブルー）&ビニーリーキオプション

人とクルマの「体感」

あらゆる速度で、一体一秒、楽しく走るための技術

もっとも、と走し　走るためのオープン

#03　リアストレーキ／各色　¥38,000

リヤタイヤハウスの後方の流れと、さらにその内側というも面という見地に触れないように設計するエアロパーツ。タイヤハウス内に引き込まれる余計な空気の流れを整えることで、リヤの......

#04　トランクスポイラー／各色　¥50,000

高速走行時の操りを押え......

#01　フロントアンダースポイラー／各色　¥50,000

#02　ライセンスフレーム（フロント専用）／¥3,000

フロントのナンバープレートを飾り、エッジを引き締めるフレーム。

#01　ソフトトップカバー／¥55,000

#02　ウインドディフレクター／¥26,000

#03　シフトノブ（チタン製）／¥15,000

#04　ニーパッド／¥30,000

#05　ブレーキパッド（ノンアスベストタイプ／フロント・リアセット）／¥40,000

スポーツ走行でのS2000の運動性をシャープに引き出してくれるブレーキ性能を追求。

The most important pages from the original accessories catalogue, with bodykit components, the windblocker, titanium gearknob and kneepads being highlighted. Note the holes in the right-hand pad, allowing the speakers to remain efficient.

Honda's proposed F1 machine for the 2000 season, seen at the 1999 Tokyo Motor Show. Sadly, the RA-099 project was to be stillborn, following the sudden death of the car's designer. Honda ultimately returned to the Formula One scene via BAR, eventually taking over Mugen's role as an engine supplier to other teams as well.

THE NEW CAR IN AMERICA

US sales started in September 1999, a few months behind those of the domestic market. The company was aiming to move 5000 cars in the States during the first year (or MY, to be more accurate), but the target had almost been reached by the time January 2000 came along – there was certainly no need to wait until the end of the 2000 season to start popping champagne corks in Torrance, California, Honda's spiritual home in North America.

Naturally, in an age of 'world car' specifications, the US-bound model was very similar to the S2000 sold in Japan. But there were differences, including a few fairly significant ones. For starters, the compression ratio was set at 11.0:1 rather than 11.7, meaning a slight reduction in power (quoted at 240bhp) and only 153lbft of torque – a loss of 7lbft compared to the domestic vehicles.

Official paperwork states the US machines were 15mm (0.6in) shorter than Japanese ones, but this was only the lack of a mandatory front registration plate accounting for the difference; the rear number plate area was much the same. The lighting looked similar, although internal configurations and wiring had to be adjusted to suit Federal rules, and the combination indicator and side marker units in the headlights were orange, rather than white with amber bulbs. American cars also had rubber guides ahead of the wheels, and tyres with a higher speed rating beyond them; careful inspection also revealed the use of different alloy wheels compared to those fitted to the S2000 in Japan, Europe and Australia.

Standard equipment levels were higher, meaning a fraction more weight to contend with, although, strangely, fewer coachwork colours were offered (black, silver, red and white shades only). However, unlike the Japanese cars (and European and Australasian models, for that matter), which had the Honda 'H' badge on the nose and tail filled with coloured resin to match the bodywork on the early cars, those shipped to the States had a hollow relief badge – more of a pain when it came to cleaning, but doubtless more stylish in appearance, and less of a burden when it came to stocking spares as well.

Apart from the engine tuning, all other leading mechanical specifications were carried over from the JDM model. Stock features on the $32,000 base car included a power soft top, HID headlights, cast aluminium alloy wheels, EPS, ABS, intermittent wipers, power mirrors, power windows, remote control locking, air-conditioning, cruise control, a CD/radio unit with two speakers, an aluminium gearknob, leather seats, a leather-trimmed steering wheel, storage boxes and cup holder, and a 12V power socket. There were no factory options offered initially, but that's hardly surprising, and only a handful of dealer accessories, such as the folding windblocker and floormats.

The Wall Street Journal carried an interesting piece in mid-November 1999, stating: "Some will find the Honda roadster provides more race car sensation than they bargained for. Driving it smoothly requires more than the usual dose of concentration. Engine speed has to be kept in the 'power band' to achieve snappy performance, which calls for frequent stirring of the six-speed gearbox.

"The car's stiff suspension helps it grip the road and dart through tight curves with breathtaking speed. But it also makes the tiny car feel twitchy at times and can

(Continues page 60)

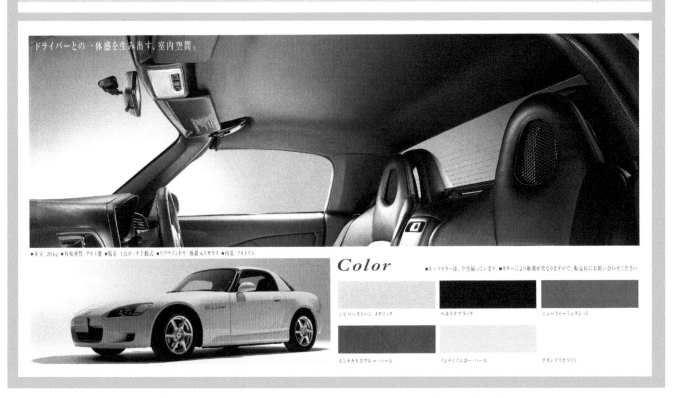

Flyer for the attractive new hardtop. Being made from aluminium, it was extremely light.

A different view of the S2000 with a hardtop in place.

A red S2000 for the American market, complete with the correct badging. Several early PR shots show the JDM nose and tail badges, which were never used in the States.

Virtually all the major publishing houses in Japan produced a special edition 'mook' to celebrate the arrival of the S2000. This is the one put together by XaCar, featuring the delightful Kumi Sato on the cover. By the way, those overalls are not for show – this lady is quite a racer ...

rattle occupants who don't brace themselves for bumps ... Still, sports car purists are likely to conclude that a little bruising is a small price to pay for the S2000's brand of entertainment."

Most of the automotive magazines had already covered the newcomer in previews to such an extent that production car tests became something of a rarity in this area of the press. However, *Motor Trend* revisited the S2000 in its February 2000 issue, with the torque-loving C. van Tune noting: "Combine all that high-revving go-power with close ratio gearing and a mere 2809lb kerb weight, and Honda's new playtoy should be quite a thrill.

(Continues page 65)

This page and overleaf: Various views of a US-spec car in Silverstone Metallic with the early style red leather trim. This selection includes the engine bay, as well as a rare shot of the soft top in its raised position. Note the rear window design, which employed a plastic insert at this time (later cars adopted a glass rear screen).

This page and overleaf: The first US catalogue, which folded out to give a huge picture of a silver car on the whole of one side. The same pic was used elsewhere, so is not shown in full here.

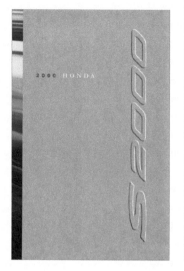

2000 HONDA

S2000

S2000

The engine start button says it all. The Honda S2000 is different. Its physical presence immediately captures the imagination. Its technical perfection is to be admired, its capabilities to be enjoyed. A car that responds to your every command as if it were a part of your body. Precise controls, superb balance, sensational performance. It's time for some serious fun.

See the S2000 redline at 9000 rpm on an informative Digital Instrument Panel™ that's much like the ones used in modern racing cars.

The S2000 interior is modeled after a Formula One race-car cockpit. After all, the idea is the same. Place the controls where you can use them. Instinctively. And design instruments so you can read them. Instantly.

Put the top down. Find an open stretch of road. Relax. It's easy to get carried away in the S2000. There's an AM/FM stereo with CD player, air conditioning, cruise control and the convenience of a remote entry system and power windows, door locks and mirrors. Your comfort is important. So is your safety. The integrated roll bars and even the strengthened windshield posts connect to reinforced frame members. And the 3-point seat belts have pretensioners.

Racing-Inspired Seats have extra back and shoulder support to better hold you in place when cornering.

The sexy Aluminum Knob invites you to shift the close-ratio six-speed to your heart's content.

thrill

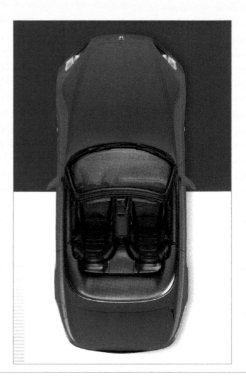

focused

High-performance technology usually trickles down from racing cars to street cars; with the S2000, it was a flood. Its 2.0 liter, 16-valve VTEC™ engine redlines at an incredible 9000 rpm, and produces 240 horsepower and 153 lb.-ft. of torque, yet it's classified as a Low-Emission Vehicle (LEV).

With its stunning looks and technical credentials, the Honda S2000 truly is a tribute to both the science and art of driving.

The Braking System features large, 11-inch, 4-wheel disc brakes that are vented in front, rigid calipers and highly fade-resistant pad material.

Designed for high-rpm operation, the engine's DOHC valvetrain uses low-friction rollerbearing cam followers. VTEC (variable valve-timing and lift electronic control) spreads power over the engine's entire operating range.

The advanced High X-Bone Frame and Monocoque Body form a tight, flex-free structure that contributes to the S2000's dynamic performance and safety.

details

Engine

Type: Aluminum-Alloy In-Line 4 with Fiber-Reinforced (FRM) Cylinder Walls

Displacement (cc/cu. in.)	1997/121.9
Horsepower @ rpm (SAE net)	240 @ 8300
Torque (lb.-ft. @ rpm)	153 @ 7500
Compression Ratio	11.0:1

Valve Train: 16-Valve DOHC VTEC™
Fuel System: Multi-Point Programmed Fuel Injection (PGM-FI)
Ignition System: Electronic with Immobilizer Theft-Deterrent System

Drivetrain

Type: Front Engine/Rear-Wheel Drive
6-Speed Manual Transmission with Torque-Sensing Limited-Slip Differential

Final Drive Ratio	4.1:1

Body/Suspension/Chassis

High X-Bone Monocoque Frame
Suspension: Independent In-Wheel Double Wishbone

Stabilizer Bar (mm, front/rear)	28.2/27.2

Coaxial Electric Power Rack-and-Pinion Steering

Steering Wheel Turns, Lock-to-Lock	2.4
Turning Diameter, Curb-to-Curb (ft.)	35.4

Power-Assisted 4-Wheel Disc Brakes

Anti-Lock Braking System (ABS)	3-Channel
Wheels (front/rear)	16x6.5JJ / 16x7.5JJ
Tires (front/rear)	P205/55 R16 89W / P225/50 R16 92W

Exterior Dimensions

Wheelbase (in.)	94.5
Length (in.)	162.2
Height (in.)	50.6
Width (in.)	68.9
Track (in., front/rear)	57.9/59.4
Curb Weight (lbs.)	2809

Interior Dimensions

Headroom (in.)	34.6
Legroom (in.)	44.3
Shoulder Room (in.)	50.2
Hiproom (in.)	49.8
Cargo Volume (cu. ft.)	5.0
Passenger Volume (cu. ft.)	48.4

Exterior Features

Electrically Powered Soft Top
Dual Outlet Exhaust
High-Intensity Discharge Headlights (HID)
Lightweight Alloy Wheels
Body-Colored Dual Power Mirrors
Remote Entry System
Impact-Absorbing Body-Colored Bumpers

Interior Features

Dual Airbags (SRS)
Power Windows
Power Door Locks
Cruise Control
Map Lights
Air Conditioning
Micron Air-Filtration System
AM/FM Stereo CD Player
Remote-Operated Audio Controls
Digital Instrument Panel
Aluminum Shift Knob
Leather-Trimmed Seats
Leather-Wrapped Steering Wheel
Center Console Storage Compartment with Lock
Beverage Holder
2-Speed/Intermittent Windshield Wipers
3-Point Seat Belts with Pretensioners
Integrated Roll Bars
Immobilizer Theft-Deterrent System
Low-Fuel Indicator Light
Engine Start Button
12-Volt Power Outlet

EPA Mileage Estimates*/Fuel Capacity

6-Speed Manual (City/Highway)	20/26
Fuel (gal.)	13.2

New Formula Red Available with Black Leather

Berlina Black Available with Black or Red Leather

Silverstone Metallic Available with Black or Red Leather

Grand Prix White Available with Red Leather

Another view of the red car shown earlier; this time augmented by a shot of its black interior.

And it is, if you're willing to drive it like a boy racer.

"Case in point: At our test track, this red S2000 was the quickest such car we've tested, racing 0-60 in 5.2 seconds and nailing the quarter-mile in 13.8. That's quick in anyone's book. But the methods required to perform such feats are nothing anyone over age 25 (mentally) is going to want to do to his own car. To extract even 75 per cent of its full performance, you have to 'treat it like you hate it.' Unfortunately, you have to do just that to really scoot. In every other way (handling, braking, ride, styling, quality and creature comforts), the S2000 is a home run. It's also a stout value."

Lining up alongside the Accord, Civic, Prelude, Insight, CR-V, Passport and Odyssey in Honda showrooms (despite rumours that it may become a stablemate for the NSX, the S2000 was kept out of the upmarket Acura brand line-up), the new car duly made it into the hallowed *Car & Driver* '10 Best' list, and was also awarded the 'Best of What's New' title by *Popular Science*. In addition, the hard chargers at *MotorWeek* named the S2000 the

S2000

Born of the closed circuit.
Destined for the open road.

S2000 instrument gauges (U.S. model shown).

The S2000 features a 6-speed manual transmission which allows for fast, controlled shifts. The clutch has a light, precise action while the brakes operate with a direct, firm feel that enhances braking control.

The engine start button says it all. The Honda S2000 is different. Serious and fun. Its technical perfection is to be admired; its capabilities – to be enjoyed. Top down, an open road, the sun and wind. A car that responds to your commands as if it were an extension of your body. Precise controls, superb balance, sensational performance. A tribute to both the science and art of driving.

Its 2.0 litre, 16-valve VTEC engine redlines at an incredible 9000 rpm, and produces 240 horsepower. That's an amazing 120 horsepower per litre—the highest power output per litre of any normally aspirated automobile engine in the world.

The S2000 interior, modeled after a Formula One race-car cockpit, connects the driver to the car. The controls are placed to be readily at hand. Instinctively. And the instruments are designed so you can read them. Instantly. Even the seats have extra back and shoulder support to better hold you in place while cornering.

The double-page S2000 section in the 2000 MY range catalogue for the Canadian market. The Silverstone Metallic car below is actually the main illustration in the US fold-out brochure.

'Best Performance Car' in its annual awards, and *Ward's* singled out the engine for praise.

EUROPEAN EXPORTS
As a breed, sporting machines have always had a strong following in Europe. After all, one can say the LWS was born there, with the likes of MG and Austin-Healey leading the way for decades. The revival of the lightweight sports car genre, ironically thanks to Japan's

Mazda MX-5 more than anything, fostered a perfect breeding ground for makers to strut their stuff, and one would probably be right in saying that the S2000 had almost come too late. One can definitely say the market had become a lot more competitive than it had been at the start of the 1990s, that's for sure, with the Honda having to fight against the BMW Z3, Mercedes-Benz SLK, Porsche Boxster, Alfa Romeo Spider, Fiat Barchetta, MGF, Toyota MR-S (bringing the MR2 up-to-date), the second

(Continues page 70)

HONDA

Honda S2000

Cover and selected pages from the first full UK catalogue, which was quite a heavyweight publication. Much of the artwork was retouched for lhd markets. (Pages 67-69)

First man, then machine

Race car design
chassis and suspension

Virtually every component in the Honda S2000 is unique to the model and the engineers set themselves the task of defining the ideal layout - in terms of chassis, suspension and the siting of the transmission - for a two-seater roadster. A solution that would excite the most demanding of drivers.

Chassis and suspension
Rigidity is a key element in the make-up of a world-class chassis. When the vehicle concerned is open top, achieving high levels of stiffness requires innovative engineering solutions. The conventional design route would be to add hefty reinforcement to an existing chassis, which was probably originally designed as a fixed-roof car. It is hard to imagine a more unsatisfactory or inelegant approach, adding weight, blunting performance and struggling with the resulting shortcomings.

The pursuit of rigidity is, of course, not just to prevent bodyshell shudder. A stiff platform allows the car's suspension and steering to operate correctly: twisting and flexing reduces the accuracy of the steering, unsettles the ride and can affect traction and, perhaps most importantly, handling precision.

The company's engineers, however, ensured that a radically new solution was developed for this age old problem of building a rigid open-top car. The answer became known as the 'high X-bone frame'.

10990T-GS0XB high X-bone chassis.

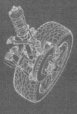

Responsive handling
chassis and suspension

The Honda S2000's high X-bone chassis is based around three large, stiff box sections: the centre tunnel and the two sills. The latter are enormously strong, wide and tall - as tall as the centre tunnel, hence the 'high' in high X-bone. These sills are joined to the centre tunnel by four rigid cross members. Two run forward into the engine bay and two run from behind the cockpit: the 'X' of the X-bone.

The result is a chassis that equals the stiffness of some otherwise fixed-head cars.

Suspension solution
With a confidence that the Honda S2000 drivetrain would be hooked up to a class-leading roadster structure, the company could confidently invest in a brand new and forward-thinking suspension system. It can be summed up in one word: precision.

Double-wishbone suspension has long been a Honda signature and the basic principle is again exploited. It is a particularly pure engineering solution, being both compact and rigid. It also ensures the wheels move up and down at right angles to the road surface, keeping the maximum amount of tyre tread on the tarmac in all circumstances.

The engineers decided to design a new system - inspired by the NSX - that was even more compact and have rigid than existing set-ups. The result was the in-wheel double wishbone which suspends the Honda S2000 from all four corners. By shrinking the whole wishbone layout and going to great lengths to specially shape the components, most of it is accommodated within the 16" alloy wheels.

Shorter wishbones mounted closer together provide a more rigid suspension setup. The steering axis also, with a reduced offset also results in a quicker and more precise reaction to the driver's steering input.

The Honda S2000's dampers, which sit inside the coil springs, include a separate gas reservoir. This race-bred detail means that the damper can use a bigger piston, which in turn means that the car benefits from a much-improved ride quality.

The rear tyres - 255/50 - are bigger than those used on the NSX while those at the front - 205/55 - are the same size, but both have specially developed construction and compounds. Honda and the tyre maker Bridgestone worked together to design the Potenza S02 especially for the Honda S2000.

A special place
the interior

In keeping with the purity of approach in all other aspects of the design of the Honda S2000, the exterior styling and interior layout are a reflection of Honda's pursuit of the highest possible driving performance. The exterior has been stretched around the sophisticated underpinnings, which is why the shape is a reflection of the compact in-wheel suspension and set-back front engine layout. It is also vital that the interior design is governed by function and good ergonomic practice, especially when the vehicle in question is a serious driver's car. Which is why the Honda S2000 cockpit rejects gimmicky looks for forward-thinking function.

In a true performance car the seating position is extremely important. By placing the seats low, the driver has a proximity to the heart of the chassis that results in a feeling of 'oneness' when driving the Honda S2000. Feeling so closely connected to a car is what allows the driver to understand the chassis: input can be more accurately delivered and the chassis' reactions can be easily and quickly understood, especially when driving hard. The low-set seats and high-point sills and doors also engender a feeling of security and close connection with the car.

Honda's commitment to redefining the performance roadster was so focused that no existing components - switchgear or instrumentation - were considered. This completely fresh look at how a driver operates in a high-performance environment throw up such a fundamental reworking of the typical cabin, that the Honda S2000 stands out as an ergonomic benchmark.

Honda's inspiration comes from motorsports like Formula One, where the driver has to be able to assimilate information and operate all the controls instantly and preferably without taking their hands from the wheel. Figuring that the same applied to a serious and skilled driver, the designers decided to locate almost all of the switchgear within fingertip distance of the steering wheel, as well as improving the at-a-glance clarity of the instrumentation. The result is a marked departure in automotive cabin design with the bonus of a race car inspired starter button mounted by the steering wheel.

Pure sports feel
the interior

At each side of the wheel are two pods, each topped with an air vent. On the left hand pod are the heating and air conditioning controls; on the right, the audio controls and the engine starter button. Between them is the digital instrument pack, semi-circular so it follows the shape of the wheel's rim. The operational logic is implicit. The direction and temperature of the heater is controlled by rotating knobs and the fan speed by a sequential rocker switch. Air conditioning and recirculation activation is by push-push switches.

Pressing the 'audio' knob switches between CD* and radio, rocking from left to right scrolls up and down through stations or tracks. Another sequential rocker switch controls the volume. Under the audio knob is the large, red starter button. This is sheer 'theatre': twist the ignition key, then press the button. It's a race car ritual.

The switch to digital instruments is equally well thought out. The rev counter is rendered as an arc around the top edge of the binnacle. It retains one of the advantages of the conventional needle: being able to 'see' the car's acceleration as the indicator 'sweeps' towards the red-line.

Under the arc the speedo displays large red numerals which are easier to read at a glance than a needle and tiny numbers. For all its functional simplicity, the Honda S2000 is not without its flourishes: an aluminium gearknob, foot pedals, beautiful leather Momo wheel, aluminium kick plates and sculpted leather sport seats.

The only switchgear not dash-mounted sits on the centre console. The hazard and headlamp washer switches are by the gearlever as is the activation for the electric hood. Like everything about the Honda S2000, this is beautifully designed, raising itself in just six seconds.

High performance
active and passive safety

The main safety benefit in building a responsive roadster is that the inherent responsiveness can be used to avoid potentially dangerous incidents as well as deliver a thrilling drive. The rigidity of the high X-bone chassis, for example, is more than just an ideal basis for the sophisticated suspension; it also delivers exceptional impact protection.

Because the central section of the steel monocoque is very stiff, it allows the Honda S2000 crumple zones to deform in a more effective and controlled manner. The fact that the car's massive box-section sills and centre tunnel are joined by substantial load-bearing members is another crucial aspect of the car's passive safety performance. In the event of a side impact, not only is the occupant protected by the sheer physical size and strength of the sill section, but also its connection to the centre tunnel means the force of the impact is transferred from the sill and into the chassis' centre tunnel.

The result is that the crash forces are routed around the occupants and absorbed by the chassis, reducing the shock experienced by the passengers. The integration of the sill and centre tunnel structure has been dubbed the 'load dispersion frame layout'.

The engineers - aided by powerful computer simulations - also used the stringent European NCAP crash test regime as a guideline when addressing the crash protection offered by the Honda S2000.

Having exercised such detailed attention to front and side impact protection, Honda was not going to ignore the potential hazard of a roll-over. Like many other roadsters, the Honda S2000 has heavily reinforced windscreen surrounds, achieved by sandwiching a steel tube made from high-strength alloy steel in between the pressings. But unlike some other roadsters, the Honda S2000 also wears heavy duty roll bars behind each seat. These internally reinforced steel loops are fixed directly to the car's chassis members, making for very secure roll-over protection.

Driver and passenger airbags are standard on the Honda S2000, as are seatbelt pretensioners, which tighten to help secure the occupants more firmly into their seats in case of impact.

Of course it's to be hoped that the Honda S2000 braking system will stop the car before any impact can take place. Despite the complexity of 'in-wheel' suspension, the engineers have managed to install massive 300 mm ventilated disc brakes on the front wheels of the car and 282 mm discs on the rear and naturally anti-lock brakes come as standard.

Front and rear views of an early left-hand drive car for mainland Europe. Coachwork colours varied from country to country across the EU, with the UK restricted to Silverstone Metallic, Ascari Red (New Formula Red, in reality) or Berlina Black only to start off with.

generation MX-5, the Lotus Elise, TVR Chimaera, Audi TT Roadster, and even the traditional Morgan. Buyers, with little to choose from as the eighties were almost coming to an end, were suddenly spoilt for choice when it came to convertibles ...

The S2000's European première came at what was to be a thrilling 69th Geneva Motor Show, which opened to the public on 11 March 1999. No less than three cars were on display on an elevated platform, with the Honda convertible being given the 'Cabrio of the Year' award at the event; a proud Uehara-san was there to take it.

Of all the markets in the EU, despite its poor reputation on the weather front, Britain has always been the chief supporter of the drophead LWS. The UK-spec model was a cross between the domestic and US machines, as it had right-hand drive and lighting much like that of the JDM car (plus a foglight mounted on the dressing piece between the exhaust pipes) but equipment levels similar to those found in the States.

The 240PS S2000 was listed at £27,995 (compared with £69,590 for an NSX) when UK sales officially began at the end of May 1999 (orders had started being taken as early as 1 April, as it happens, although the pricing was still unknown at that time), and came with JDM-style 16in alloy wheels, HID headlights, headlight washers, a power hood with cover, power mirrors,

power windows, air-conditioning, black or red leather trim, a leather-wrapped steering wheel, an aluminium gearlever, a radio/cassette unit with two speakers and a 'bee sting' aerial, remote central locking and an immobiliser as standard. Options were basically the same as elsewhere, with bodykit components, a windblocker, floormats, a CD-changer, rear utility net

This is actually one of the images that was reserved and retouched for the UK catalogue; here the car is shown as a left-hand drive model. Note the rear foglight underneath the number plate.

(for behind the seats) and body cover being amongst them.

Pricing had increased to £28,545 (about twice the cost of a sporty Civic) by the spring of 2000. The sticker price was dropped almost ten per cent soon after, and not because of outside influences, which is interesting. *Autocar* may have hit the nail on the head a year earlier: "When you're driving the car very hard and getting every inch of performance out of its incredible engine, you'd say that the S2000 is decently priced. But when you're not using it this hard – a large percentage of the time – you could be in an MX-5 which cost you £10,000 less."

Although the magazine had high expectations of the newcomer, the question of practicality in an era of speed cameras and congested roads had to be faced up to. There were also things like the level of buffeting (the test car didn't have a windblocker fitted) and the lack of adjustment in the steering column that raised eyebrows. But the main problem was the focused nature of the beast, appealing only to a narrow band of serious enthusiasts rather than the masses. It was a niche market car surrounded by worthy competitors that offered all manner of benefits in a far wider range of situations.

THE S2000 IN THE ANTIPODES

John Lamm tried two of the three pre-production prototypes (the third one had been written-off by a journalist!), and writing in *Wheels* magazine stated: "Honda had a Boxster and Z3 on hand for comparison driving. After the S2000, the Porsche felt almost soft and too well tamed when driven mildly, though it comes into its own as the speed rises. The BMW Z3 seemed slightly and not badly vintage, particularly with the space you turn off on-centre before its renowned

Press shots showing a pair of early cars for the Australian market – much the same as the UK-spec model, including the alloy wheel design, but without the rear foglight.

リアルコンフォート S2000
http://www.spoonsports.co.jp

十勝24時間耐久レース

初挑戦のニュルブルクリンク24時間レースに
完走した4週間後、スプーンは今度は十勝24
時間にS2000を送り込み、ここでも完走を
果たしました。自分たちが自信をもって選んだ
「いいクルマ」を、もっといいクルマに仕立て
て、そのクルマを愛する人々に存分にドライビ
ングを楽しんでもらいたい。スプーンはそう考
えて耐久レースに挑んでいるのです。それにし
ても、1周25kmのニュルブルクリンクの苛酷
さは想像を大きく超えていました。けれど、そ
れを身をもって体験したことで、新たなステッ
プが見えてきました。手に汗握ることなしにニ
ュルを楽しめるS2000。それがリアルコン
フォートを目指すスプーンの次の目標なのです。

「2つの24時間から学んだこと」

ニュルブルクリンク24時間耐久レース

■SPOON S2000をより深く知っていただくためのビデオ+カタログを用意。

SPOON SPORTS
株式会社スプーン 〒167-0051 東京都杉並区荻窪5-2-8 TEL03-3220-3411 FAX03-3220-0970

A Spoon Sports advert showing the firm's entry in the 2000 Nürburgring 24-hour Race. The team then competed in the Tokachi 24-hour event (upper picture) in Hokkaido, Japan's north island.

In the background, 2000 was not so good for the F1 teams, and although Honda lost out on the Indycar manufacturers' title, there was some consolation in the fact that Gil de Ferran won the drivers' championship. In 2001, the BAR and Jordan teams were still running with Honda power, but not achieving the desired results; it seemed that no-one could break Ferrari's domination. At least Honda won the Indy title, and claimed its 500th motorcycle GP win, and the NSX was still competitive in the domestic JGTC series. As it happens, the NSX had received a face-lift at the end of 2001, with fixed projector headlights readily identifying the latest cars.

Although not really a track warrior as such, Spoon Sports helped give the S2000 a swift race debut along with some local entries at the 2000 Nürburgring 24-hour Race, held at the end of June that year. The team finished the German classic in 32nd (but first in Class thanks to some sterling driving from Tetsu Ikuzawa and his pals), and the S2000 has been a firm favourite for Nürburgring 24-hour entrants ever since – a proper race that tests car and driver to the limits, but, unlike so many top class events nowadays, still realistic in terms of cost – with several Class wins being picked up along the way. Later German catalogues even featured some of these Honda racers.

The S2000 was also spotted racing in the Suzuka 1000km Race in the early part of the new millennia, but it was never particularly competitive at this level. Amazingly, there has never been an S2000 entered in the JGTC (later named the Super GT series), as most Honda runners insisted on using the NSX in both the GT500 and GT300 categories. Spoon Sports prepared several modified GT cars for the Super Taikyu endurance

steering comes into play. Compared with this pair, the Honda seemed almost tense – not nervous but certainly more up on its toes than the other two. Just as delightful as the S2000's mighty engine is the car's price ..."

Indeed, on sale from August 1999 with a list price of $69,950 (reduced to $68,450 during the 2000 season), the six-speed Honda represented very good value, especially considering leather trim, air-conditioning and a stereo came as part of the standard package. It was available in New Formula Red, Berlina Black, Grand Prix White, Silverstone Metallic and Monte Carlo Blue Pearl from the off, with metallic paint costing $259 extra. A total of 596 cars were sold Down Under during the first year, including around 400 that were ordered before sales officially began.

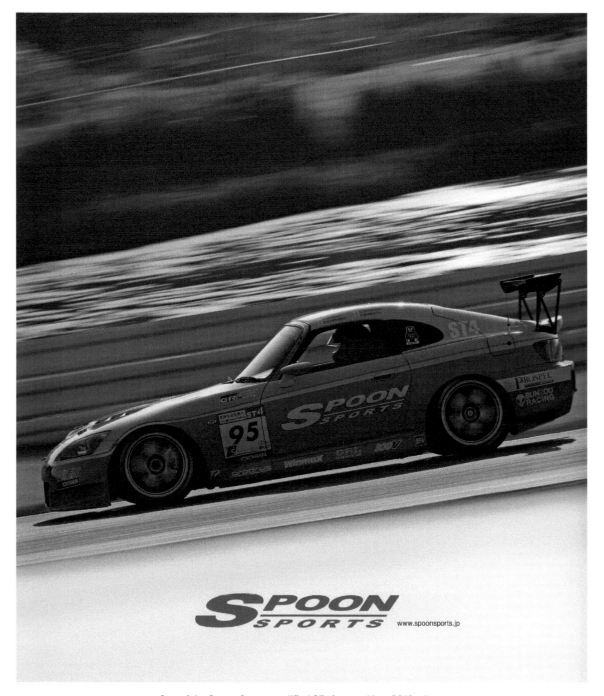

One of the Spoon Sports modified GTs featured in a 2016 advert.

series, although, to be fair, the Integra Type-R and Civic Type-R are the darlings of the track in this arena. The Tracy Sports equipe was the best S2000 team as far as results are concerned, winning the series with ease in 2014.

While there may be many Honda S2000s racing in Japan and elsewhere (the car is hugely popular with SCCA racers in the States, for instance), they tend to be used in events that are not international level, and therefore can't really be branded as justification for stoking up a pukka competition history for the model. The S2000 was evolving nicely as a road car, though ...

Record of
the early machines

With the S2000 now safely launched in each of the world's major markets, it was time to let the vehicle mature ...

With an EPA rating of 20/26, the 2001 S2000 was priced at $32,300 in the States – a fraction more than before, but certainly nothing to lose sleep over, especially considering that the windblocker and floormats were now standard fitments. An emergency trunk release was made part of the 2001 package, doubtless thwarting the plans of would-be kidnappers everywhere, yellow paintwork could be specified, the removable aluminium hardtop became available as an option (in dealerships from mid-January 2001, priced at $2995), and a clock was also included as something new in the catalogue's features list.

The NSX had a clock from day one, so it's a pretty lame excuse to say a driver's car didn't need one (the official line). In reality, most stereo units from the period came with this, and one can assume it was taken for granted in the design phase. The fact that the audio lid hides the stereo most of the time, and makes it awkward to see even when raised, is a moot point, of course, but at least a clock was now on the spec sheet. Even here, though, we need some clarification. A clock was standard on American cars, albeit via the adoption of a new stereo – JDM buyers had to do without one until the 2002 MY minor change, unless they invested in the navi system or a different head unit.

Dealer options included an alarm, CD-changer unit, a titanium shift lever, and the various bodykit components offered in Japan. Minor items included net seatback pockets, a cargo net for the boot, locking wheelnuts, and a dedicated car cover.

HOME MARKET REVISIONS
The 2001 season started early in Japan, for 14 July 2000 witnessed the S2000 Type V go on sale. Priced at 3,560,000 yen (against 3,380,000 yen for the strict S2000 model), the main difference was in the steering system, for the Type V was fitted with an electronically-controlled VGS (variable gear-ratio steering) rack.

Although quite common nowadays, Honda's VGS was a real trailblazer at the time, and perfectly suited to sports car applications. Steplessly varying the gear ratio according to vehicle speed and steering angle, the VGS-equipped car came with a steering setup that featured a remarkably fast 1.4 turns lock-to-lock. Reactions to driver input became noticeably sharper on winding roads, giving the feeling of immediate response and quick turn-in. On the other hand, steering sensitivity was automatically reduced, whilst cruising on highways and so on, in order to enhance stability.

As well as a special steering wheel, the Type V employed fresh dampers with modified rebound springs to increase damping force, as well as tweaks to the anti-roll bar and limited-slip differential settings. One of the problems was that the VGS system added 20kg (44lb) to the kerb weight, and Japanese track tests from the time showed that the standard car was actually faster. Magazines like *Car Graphic* were also critical of the steering feel, noting that EPS was hardly the best thing for a sports car in the first place, but with VGS, even more communication with the road was lost. Many questioned the worth of the costly gimmick as a result, and sales of the Type V grade were ultimately relatively slow.

The innovative VGS steering rack.

2001 Honda S2000

S2000

Maybe it's the engine start button. Or that big "9" staring back at you from the end of the tach. Something about the S2000 tells you this is no ordinary two-seater. This is all about race-bred performance and g-forces. And that's why you're here. Driving the S2000 is the exhilaration and technology extracted from Honda's 50 years of racing experience. With 240 horsepower and a lofty 9000-rpm redline, it's the first roadster to capture the soul of racing. A few seconds behind the wheel will explain it all.

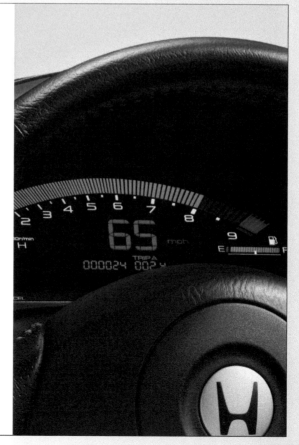

The majority of the 2001 S2000 catalogue for the US market, avoiding duplication. (pages 75-78)

possessed

Under the hood, a genie wants out of its bottle.

You don't have to believe in magic. But it may help. The 2.0-liter engine in the Honda S2000 produces 240 horsepower and 153 lb.-ft. of torque. That's an amazing 120 horsepower per liter, the highest specific output of any normally aspirated production engine in the world. Yet it runs so clean, the S2000 qualifies as a Low-Emission Vehicle (LEV). The explanation for this virtuosity can be found on the racetracks of the world. Honda racing technology courses through the veins of the S2000. From its 16-valve VTEC™ engine, redlining at an incredible 9000 rpm, to its close-ratio 6-speed manual transmission, which lets you accelerate quickly in any gear. This rear-wheel-drive S2000 also has a torque-sensing limited-slip differential to ensure plenty of grip. All contained in a masterfully rigid, high X-bone frame for unequalled handling precision and stability.

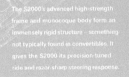

The large 11-inch 4-wheel disc brakes are vented in front and solid in back, with a highly fade-resistant pad material. Pedal feel and brake bias are specifically designed for hard braking. An anti-lock braking system (ABS) is standard.

The S2000's advanced high-strength frame and monocoque body form an immensely rigid structure - something not typically found in convertibles. It gives the S2000 its precision-tuned ride and razor-sharp steering response.

A suspension programmed to hug the road.

The contact patch, where the tire meets the pavement, is where a car's performance has its moment of truth. The compact "in-wheel" design of the S2000's 4-wheel double wishbone suspension is dedicated to maximizing grip and precision. High-strength suspension components are light and compact, reducing unsprung weight for excellent control. The rear-wheel-drive S2000 uses front and rear stabilizer bars and gas-pressurized, mono-tube shock absorbers to help minimize body roll and ride harshness. The integrity of the S2000 results in agility and handling response that must be felt to be properly appreciated. You feel the road, but leave the bumps behind.

To lower the center of gravity, the engine and transmission are positioned low in the chassis, behind the front suspension.

Innovative, technically sophisticated for its day and a truly enjoyable car to drive, the S600 was one of Honda's very first sports cars.

inspired

In 1963, the Honda Motor Company entered Formula 1 racing. Since then, Honda has continued to compete at many of the highest levels of international motorsports, winning 71 Grand Prix, 6 Formula 1 Constructor's Championships, 3 Championship Auto Racing Teams (CART) Manufacturer's Championships and more than 80 races in the series. The S2000 roadster carries on this racing spirit.

Tap into a rich legacy of performance engineering.

Racing isn't just about crowds and trophies. For Honda, the racing program is an opportunity to put new performance technology to the test in extreme situations. At Honda, one of the primary directives includes sending young engineers into the crucible of racing to sharpen their problem-solving skills.

The time constraints imposed by racing provide the context for learning to innovate under pressure. A racing competitor once commented that while many car companies go racing, Honda is a racing company that happens to build production cars. The S2000 embodies that passion and competitive heritage.

gripping

Forget everything you knew about roadsters.

You rotate the key in its cylinder. Then you do something new. Something racecar drivers have done for years. You press a button to start the engine. Which should remind you that this is more than a run-of-the-mill sports car. This is serious business. The aluminum shift knob for the 6-speed clicks through its paces with a flick of the wrist. The leather seats give you outstanding support, with generous leg and side bolsters. Concentrate on the business at hand—the thrill of being one with the car.

A clear acrylic aero screen fits between the driver's and passenger's seats to help reduce wind turbulence. If you prefer, it folds down out of the way.

With left-hand controls, you can change audio system modes, preset channels and volume—or route the sound quickly and easily with the touch of a fingertip.

So many rpms. So little time.

Textured pedals improve grip and provide a consistent connection to the racecar heritage of the S2000. The clutch is sprung for light, precise action, while the brakes have a direct feel that enhances braking control.

A full-bodied approach to the performance state of mind. Settle into the leather seat, adjust the seatback and slide the seat into position. The S2000 interior immerses you in the roadster experience, whether you take advantage of its race-bred performance or simply wish to take in some fresh air. The high seat bolsters brace your back and shoulders through the turns, the steering feel is precise and responsive, and the gauges mean business. The S2000 also has an easy-to-use two-latch release for its motorized top, an AM/FM stereo with CD player, electronically controlled heating and air conditioning with a micron air-filtration system, and power windows, mirrors and door locks.

The S2000 is serious about performance, but just as serious about passenger safety. The body and frame are engineered not only to hold up to the rigors of spirited driving, but also to help protect you in a full-frontal, offset-frontal, side or rear impact. There are dual front airbags¹ and 3-point seat belts with pretensioners. The driver's and passenger's integrated roll bars – and the door and windshield posts – are reinforced, and connect to frame members in the floor. The central tunnel and front and rear side-members of the X-bone frame are designed to offer the rigidity and passenger protection of a closed-top vehicle in full-frontal and rear impacts. Side-impact protection is built into the doors, side sills and cockpit floor. An Immobilizer Theft-Deterrent System gives you peace of mind when you park your S2000. And a locking storage compartment in the center console keeps small items securely out of view.

¹ Handle remote use, and your safest ways to bi-sturdy in think up.

intense

The big news for American buyers was the availability of yellow coachwork for the 2001 season.

The last time you had this much fun driving a car it cost a quarter and gyrated in front of the supermarket.

The six-speed, 240-horsepower, 0-60 in less than six seconds Honda S2000.

American advertising dating from February 2001.

On the colour palette, the Japanese 2001 MY cars (given the internal AP1-110 designation) gained Midnight Pearl as a new paintwork alternative, along with a red leather interior option.

Mid-September 2001 brought with it a new set of updates, and the launch of the AP1-120 model. This featured a whole new range of custom paintwork options (forcing Honda to adopt the 'H' badge already used in the States rather than a coloured one), a new hood, a number of exterior and interior upgrades aimed at improving quality feel, and some subtle suspension modifications to 'mature' the car's handling.

The new hood incorporated a glass rear screen with a heater and timer, ending a barrage of complaints regarding the original back window, the windscreen frame became body colour instead of black, the wheels were changed to the US-spec rims (the same size, but a slightly different

SPECIFICATIONS

The leading specifications for the early models, with the home market (JDM) base car shown as the reference vehicle. Significant differences between grades and export models, as well as running changes, are noted against each entry. Special editions are covered within the text.

Model

Code	GH-AP1 (later LA-AP1)
Type	Two-seater open car with a power-operated convertible soft top. Steel unit construction body

Engine

Code	F20C
Mounting	Front, longitudinal
Cylinders	Four, water-cooled in two-piece cast aluminium alloy block with FRM cylinder liners
Head	Cast aluminium alloy, with dohc and four valves per cylinder, plus a VTEC variable valve timing mechanism
Capacity	1997cc
Bore & stroke	87.0mm x 84.0mm
Compression ratio	11.7:1 (11.0:1 for USA and ROW)
Fuel delivery	Electronic fuel-injection (PGM-FI)
Ignition	12V electronic, distributorless, with separate coils
Power @ rpm	250PS @ 8300 (240bhp for US and ROW)
Torque @ rpm	160lbft @ 7500 (153lbft for USA and ROW)

Transmission

Gearbox type	Six-speed manual
Clutch	Single dry plate
Internal ratios	3.13, 2.04, 1.48, 1.16, 0.97 and 0.81
Reverse gear	2.80
Final-drive	4.10:1
Driven wheels	Rear, with limited-slip differential

Chassis

Front suspension	Independent, via double-wishbones, coil springs, and gas-filled tubular shock absorbers. Anti-roll bar 28.2mm (1.11in) later changed to 26.5mm (1.04in)
Rear suspension	Independent, via double-wishbones, coil springs, and gas-filled tubular shock absorbers. Anti-roll bar 27.2mm (1.07in)
Front brakes	300mm (11.8in) diameter ventilated discs, single-pot calipers, with anti-lock system (ABS)
Rear brakes	282mm (11.1in) solid discs, single-pot calipers, with anti-lock system (ABS). Mechanical handbrake mechanism included
Front wheels	Alloys, 6.5J x 16
Front tyres	205/55 VR16 (WR rating in USA and ROW)
Rear wheels	Alloys, 7.5J x 16
Rear tyres	225/50 VR16 (WR rating in USA and ROW)
Steering	Rack-and-pinion with EPS electrical power assistance
Lock-to-lock	2.4 turns, or 1.4 with VGS system

Dimensions

Wheelbase	2400mm (94.5in)
Overall length	4135mm (162.8in), or officially 4120mm (162.2in) for USA
Overall height	1285mm (50.6in)
Body width	1750mm (68.9in)
Front track	1470mm (57.9in)
Rear track	1510mm (59.4in)
Ground clearance	130mm (5.1in)
Fuel capacity	50 litres (11 Imperial gallons)
Typical weight	1240kg (2728lb), or 1260kg (2772lb) with VGS system; 1275kg (2805lb) for USA, and 1260kg (2772lb) for ROW

Press photographs for the S2000 Type V, which looked much the same as a regular S2000, apart from the unusual steering wheel and the 'VGS' badge on the tail, underneath the bootlid keyhole. The alloy wheels are the optional BBS rims, by the way.

design), the body containing the HID lights was chromed, and chrome rings were added to the rear lights.

Interior changes included a fresh gearknob in leather and aluminium, an aluminium driver's footrest, net door pockets, and a new, more powerful stereo (a radio/CD/MD unit with a clock display) and four speakers – the original two in the doors, each now having a tweeter above them. In addition, the interior colouring and centre console trim was revised, the keyless entry system was updated to include welcome lighting, and the windblocker became a standard feature (the hood cover remained an option, though).

A BF Goodrich advert spotted in Japan during the spring of 2001, showing a modified S2000. The car has been lowered, with a bodykit and large wheel and tyre combination, while the engine has had a Comptech supercharger fitted.

Exterior of the home market car, seen here in the press release images from September 2001. Note the colour-keyed windscreen frame, the new soft top design, and the chrome rings dressing the tail-lights. The sticker on the bootlid was to say the vehicle passed the contemporary local gas emissions regulations with a two-star rating. This meant the S2000 was entitled to an LA chassis code – a top three-star rating brought with it an ABA designation.

The regular S2000 was now priced at 3,430,000 yen, while the Type V commanded 3,610,000 yen. Premium paint cost 200,000 yen, with leather trim at 100,000 yen, a DVD navigation system at 220,000 yen, and BBS alloys 200,000 yen. Dealer options were much the same as before, covering everything from floormats through to Modulo body kits. If this was too tame, one could always turn to Mugen, who would extract another 15PS from the engine via a new exhaust system, a carbon-fibre airbox ahead of the radiator, a new ECU, and a fresh thermostat

(Continues page 87)

Selected pages from the rather plain 2002 MY domestic catalogue, with some of the unique coachwork and trim options available in Japan. The one for the 2003 JDM season was actually the same apart from a small reduction in the colour choices (120 combinations rather than 130).

Seat &
Interior Color

スタンダード＆インテリアはメーカーオプション

ブラック（ファブリックシート＆インテリア）
（シート地はカブロン・ファブリックのコンビ）

ブラック（本革シート＆インテリア）

レッド（本革シート）＆インテリア

ブルー（本革シート＆インテリア）

レッド（本革シート）＆ブラック（インテリア）

S2000 typeV

もっと一体感あふれる走りを。もっと気持ちにフィットするステアワークを。
より高度なスポーツハンドリングのために開発したVGSを採用したS2000 typeV。
このVGSは、クルマの車速と舵角に応じてステアリングのギア比が変化する、
市販車として世界初の、Hondaの独自技術。
例えば低速域においては、舵角の大小にかかわらずクルマはクイックに、
高速域においては、小舵角ではゆるやかに大舵角ではクイックに応答。
そのためドライバーが、クリアしたいと思うラインを予測しながらステアリングを切ると、
ギア比がバリアブルに変化して、クルマは道をトレースするように機敏かつ忠実に追従する
その一連のモーションが、ドライバーにリニアなフィールを感じさせる。

また S2000 typeVは、サスペンションシステムも専用にチューン。
それによってあらゆる速度域においてスポーティ感にあふれた
ハンドリングを楽しむことが可能に。リバウンド側の減衰力を高めながら、
リバウンドスプリングを内蔵してダンパーを前進化に採用。
スタビライザーとLSD・リミテッドスリップデフを専用化するなど、
ハイレスポンスなハンドリングに対応している

Special Parts for S2000 Hard Top

軽量アルミ製一体成形のエアロダイナミクスデザイン
両装に、頭部保護を考慮した、クッションのきいたソフトルーフを採用
ルーベを思わせる、スタイリッシュなフルトリムインテリア
着脱は4点ワーク手動式で、トップを外者なシートに身を沈めると
そこにはタイトな一体感がドライバーを待っている

Accessories

Driving Harmony.▷▷▷

Modulo
Honda Custom Performance

モデューロは、世界のトップレベルをいくホンダ車と
まったく同じ基準によって、ホンダのエンジニアが車の性能、魅力を
際立たせたオリジナル カスタマイズ・ブランド。
ホンダ純正ならではの、デザイン性、機能性、信頼性、品質保証などによって
他にはマネのできないクオリティを実現。

①シフトノブ(チタン製)
¥16,000 0.1H

●リアルチタンパネル
●ラジオリモートスイッチ+ヒーターコントロール部/ ¥18,000 0.2H
●シフトゲート+アッシュトレイ部/ ¥16,500 0.2H

④パワーウインドウ
運転席側+助手席側/ ¥12,000 0.2H

⑤ニーパッド
¥30,000 0.8H

⑥シートバックネット
¥4,000

⑦シートバックバッグ
¥8,000

⑧トランクリア
¥8,000 0.3H

ハードトップスタンド(カバー付)
¥49,500

ハードトップ収納状態

ボディカバー
●フルタイプ ¥20,000 ●ハーフタイプ ¥16,000

フルタイプ
ハーフタイプ

フロアカーペットマット(ブラック/レッド/ブルー)
●S2000用/各 ¥25,000 各0.1H
●type V用/ 各 ¥25,000 各0.1H

ブラック　レッド　ブルー

ジュニアシート(学童用シート)
¥7,500

カーアラーム
(盗難警報装置)
¥16,800 1.0H

ETC車載器
(アンテナ一体型)
¥32,300 0.4H
[ETC取付アタッチメント ¥1,500 含む]

Gather
Honda Multi Car-AV S

ギャザズは3年
6万km保証で

装着前　装着後

アクアクリーンミラー
(親水式ドアミラー/ブルー)
●左右セット ¥12,000 0.2H

●このカタログに掲載されている用品は、装着状態で車検を受けられます。●価格は取付費を含まないメーカー希望小売価格(消費税抜き)です。●□内の数字は標準取付時間です。記載の商品につきましては、別途取付費が必要です。●商品の中には同時装着できないものがあります。詳しくは販売店にお問い合わせください。
●取付費の詳細および仕様・品番・適用車種等につきましては販売店にお問い合わせください。●撮影のため、アクセサリー以外の小品を使用しています。●取付費は販売店によって異なりますので、詳しくは販売店にお問い合わせください。
●仕様および価格は予告なく変更する場合があります。●このカタログの写真は印刷のため、実際の色とは多少異なる場合があります。●このカタログに記載された価格、仕様は2001年9月現在のものです。

Home market dealer options and accessories from September 2001.

and radiator cap. Mugen could also supply wheels and tyres, as well as a number of suspension upgrades ...

THE 2002 SEASON IN THE US

As the press release stated: "Moving into its third model year on the market, demand for Honda's sporty S2000 roadster shows no signs of slowing." Indeed, with several new awards in the bag, while American Honda sales were up just over four per cent as a whole in 2001, with improved availability, US S2000 sales had rocketed by 42 per cent over the previous year.

In dealerships from the first day of November 2001, the 2002 model would further enhance the two-seater's appeal via a series of small but thoughtful upgrades. Priced at $32,400 (only $100 more than a 2001 car) and available in fresh blue and silver hues, the 2002 car came with a revised hood with a glass rear window and defroster (this silenced a string of complaints regarding the soft rear screen in the soft top from the off, while the heater elements were activated by a switch similar to the cruise control one, but on the opposite side of the steering column), chrome rings on the rear lights, a silver-grey dash panel frame with metallic-type inlays, plus a matching extended gearbox surround, stronger graphics for the digital gauges (including a white arc joining the numbers on the tachometer), a new leather and aluminium gearknob to overcome discomfort in extremes of weather, vinyl trim rather than carpeting on the upper part of the transmission tunnel, silver accents on the interior door pulls and handles, tiny nets on the lower part of the door trim, and a new footrest to match the pedal set.

There was also a more powerful stereo (with output upped from 20W to 30W), with a silver finish and built-in anti-theft feature, tweeter speakers with a silver surround were added to the top of the door cappings, and audio enthusiasts were also able to specify a Kelton Bassworks subwoofer. In addition, the standard hood boot was revised, and where the red leather trim had

Tailpiece. A Japan-only S2000 Type V for the 2002 Model Year, this example finished in Sebring Silver Metallic with a full red interior, as opposed to a black car with red seats – something one could specify in the home market.

used red door inlays on a black casing, a black fascia and a black rear storage console assembly, red now meant all-red as far as the States was concerned, along with all-blue (new for 2002) and all-black options. All these things came together to give the cockpit an altogether more inviting aura, and with no weight penalty beyond a few grams.

Away from the cosmetics, although the catalogues and press packs fail to keep abreast of the change, the front anti-roll bar diameter was reduced to 26.5mm (1.04in), while the front spring rates were increased, the rear ones decreased, and the dampers recalibrated to further improve steering feel and handling progression on the limit. Other mechanical changes included a

US MARKET AP1 COLOUR AND TRIM OPTIONS

This sidebar charts the changes in the coachwork colour and interior trim for the US-spec S2000, the date being the model year (MY) for Stateside vehicles. For the sake of completeness, notes on the Canadian market have been included, too.

2000 MY: New Formula Red, Berlina Black, Silverstone Metallic and Grand Prix White paint choices. The red shade came with black leather trim only, the black and silver hues came with black or red leather trim choices, and the white finish with red leather trim only. The hood was available in black only.

2001 MY: Spa Yellow Pearl (Indy Yellow in Japan) paintwork added, taking the body colour choices up to five, and came with black leather trim only. No other changes. However, Canadian customers were offered Monte Carlo Blue Pearl in place of Grand Prix White.

2002 MY: Silverstone Metallic replaced by Sebring Silver Metallic (same trim options). Also, Suzuka Blue Metallic (Nürburgring Blue in Japan) paintwork added, taking the body colour choices up to six, and came with blue leather trim only. No other changes, although Canada was not offered the yellow shade for this season.

2003 MY: Silverstone Metallic brought back to run alongside Sebring Silver Metallic (same trim options), taking coachwork colour choices up to seven. Tan trim added for Grand Prix White cars, replacing the existing red option; black cars lost the red interior choice, but all other trim carried over. Blue hood available as an accessory, augmenting the traditional black one. Canada was back to the four original colours, albeit with Sebring Silver covering the silver hue.

Various views of the US-spec car for the 2002 season, with the blue paintwork that was new for America in that year much in evidence, along with the fresh interior details and chrome rings on the rear lights.

tweak to the transmission to make shifts smoother and quieter, and the adoption of a beefier clutch plate. These suspension and transmission changes were also applied to cars in other markets in due course.

Car & Driver tested a new model against a bunch of its contemporaries and found: "The S2000's real charm doesn't come out until you head for a serpentine road or racetrack. There, the Honda's junior-miss mass, neutral handling, hardy brakes and hair-trigger controls make it the most fun to dust apexes with ... The S2000 was created for racetracks. The car would be much closer to perfect if a track could be rolled up and carried around in the trunk."

EUROPE & AUSTRALIA

In Britain, the aluminium hardtop became available in October 2000, coming with a heated rear screen and stand as a £1800 option. This was pretty good value, and easier to swallow with prices cut by over £2500 for the 2001 season. The basic S2000 now cost £25,995, and remained that way until the end of the 2002 Model Year.

Naturally, UK buyers (and other enthusiasts in mainland Europe, of course) were treated to the 2002 MY face-lift, but they also gained light blue and yellow paint options (still shying away from white, Monte Carlo Blue had been added for 2001, taking the total of coachwork colour choices to six, combined with black, black/red, red

Suddenly, every road's
your favorite.

Let's see, there must be
a longer way there.

The 2002 catalogue for the US market was much the same as the 2001 version, with only the odd minor change here and there, so only the pages with significant differences are shown here. Note the retouched photo of the black car, now sporting a new hood design and chrome rings on the rear lights. Who says the camera never lies?

or blue leather trim), the chance to specify a blue soft top, and a radio/CD player with a clock and four speakers. Incidentally, the screen surround became body colour at this time, as per the JDM cars, leaving only America as a main market to continue with a black frame.

The March 2002 availability of the S2000 GT had nothing to do with the suspension upgrades found in other markets. Sure, they were adopted in the UK, too, but the GT was actually a car supplied with a colour-coded removable hardtop as standard. The GT grade was listed at £26,995 – only £1000 more than the base model.

Incidentally, the Honda UK press release from 28 March 2002 mentions the adoption of "deeper and chunkier alloy wheels" in the text. This point is usually missed by enthusiasts, for the rims look much the same at first glance. However, on checking the spares book, the wheels were indeed given a new part number. This is because, like Japan, Europe had decided to adopt the US-style alloy wheel for the 2002 face-lift!

Australia followed Britain's lead. The 2001 model S2000 was launched in January that year, priced at $75,249, meaning an increase of about ten per cent over

Press shot of the UK car for the 2002 season. Note the body-coloured windscreen surround, silvered HID headlight housings, and new nose badge.

Yellow paint was available in Australia during 2001, but the colour-coded windscreen frame and headlight design shows this to be a 2002 model. Like this example, some of the early 2002 cars sent Down Under continued to sport the old nose and tail badges.

Another Australian model with the 2002 face-lift components in place, but playing a rather more active role for the driver ...

the previous season. Indy Yellow Pearl paint was added to the colour charts, giving six choices for Aussie buyers, and the hardtop was introduced at $6562.

February 2002 saw the release of the face-lifted S2000, priced at $74,990. Like Britain and mainland Europe, the changes first seen in Japan in September 2001 were adopted (taking in items like the new hood, wheels, suspension revisions, and exterior and interior cosmetic upgrades), with Nürburgring Blue Metallic paint added at the same time.

2003 Honda
$2000

Racy roadster. Ever dream of piloting machine? The engine whines, rubber b your breath as G-forces pin you to your se one with the car. Heart-pounding, adren hard-charging excitement is the spiri S2000, backed up by th more than 70 Formula One since 1964 and over 50 victories in the CA open-wheel racing series. The desire to w and a rich 40-year racing heritage insp the DNA of the S2000, a showcase of Hon technology. Get ready for a blistering sta

THE 2003 SEASON

The car for the American market was basically unchanged. Priced at $32,600 (6MT only), about the only thing of note was the revised coachwork and interior colour options, which are outlined in the sidebar on page 88, and the availability of a blue hood, bought as an accessory. This is as good a place as any given the last statement to say that any soft top colour other than black or blue is definitely not an OEM item.

Non-standard cars abound nowadays, of course, as the S2000 was ripe for tuning. While the stock model was getting softer (like the original FD-type RX-7, for most folks it was ultimately more of a track machine than something to go shopping in), tuners everywhere were in a frenzy: supercharging, turbocharging, intercooling, dressing up, stiffening up, and lowering the Honda two-seater. The author has even seen cars fitted with lift-up doors, hinged close to the screen pillars! *Fast & Furious* has a lot to answer for ...

The March 2003 edition of *Road & Track* covered one such modified vehicle, and while I don't want to touch the tuning side to any extent – a second or third volume would be needed just to get started on the subject – this one is worth mentioning, as it was from Modulo, and therefore Honda itself. The car was fitted with a five-way adjustable suspension, uprated brakes, and 17in alloys shod with Yokohama Advan rubber. Compared to the showroom model, the testers were able to shave 0.6 seconds off a lap of Willow Springs. Although not available officially in America, and the bodykit was still a prototype for show purposes, most of the mechanical bits could be bought through Honda dealers back in Japan.

There were no meaningful changes in Europe either. Germany had seen annual sales rise from 159 units in 1999 to 1478 in 2000. This was ultimately the peak, for they then dropped to 745, then 686 (opposed to over 11,000 units of the new Jazz/Fit, and only about ten per cent of Mazda MX-5 sales), and just 441 for 2003. Interestingly, for 2003, Germany had the same six standard coachwork colours as the UK, but Lime Green, Monza Red and Imola Orange were available to order,

Most of the earlier artwork was recycled once more for the US 2003 MY catalogue. These are the only real differences of note found in the latest brochure. Note the US market continued with a black windscreen frame, and failed to adopt the bright finish in the headlights, too.

SILVERSTONE METALLIC S2000 SHOWN WITH
DEALER INSTALLED FRONT UNDER
BODY SPOILER, SIDE STRAKES
AND TRUNK SPOILER.

SEBRING SILVER METALLIC S2000
SHOWN WITH DEALER INSTALLED
TRUNK SPOILER,
SIDE STRAKES
AND HARDTOP.

GRAND PRIX WHITE S2000 SHOWN WITH DEALER INSTALLED
FRONT UNDER BODY SPOILER, TRUNK SPOILER
AND HARDTOP.

Left and opposite: The 2003 US accessories catalogue for the S2000 model.

matched with black, beige, black/red or blue trim, and a black or blue soft top.

Meanwhile, in Britain, by the summer of 2003, the strict S2000 was fetching £26,000, while the S2000 GT was listed at £27,000 – both prices being just five quid up on the start of the year, as the car was basically unchanged. In Australia, a sticker price of $74,590 meant it was actually a fraction cheaper than before. Again, though, there were no significant changes to the spec sheet.

BLUE SOFT TOP

SIDE STRAKES

CARGO NET

HARDTOP STORAGE RACK

HARDTOP COVER

SEAT BACK POCKET

TRUNK SPOILER

CD CHANGER

FRONT UNDER BODY SPOILER

SECURITY SYSTEM

HONDA ACCESSORIES

The Modulo-modified car that Road & Track tested. The bodykit was produced for show purposes (close inspection will reveal several subtle differences compared to the optional appendages illustrated in the accessories catalogue), but with the S2000 face-lift due soon, there was no point in furthering the design. The styling on the kit that was actually marketed for 2004 was very aggressive ...

S2000

No other sports car can present the performance credentials of the S2000. At **240 hp**, its engine puts out more power per liter than any normally aspirated production car. And its 6-speed manual gearbox and 4-wheel double wishbone suspension reflect 40 years of Honda *racing wisdom*.

S2000 shown in Sebring Silver Metallic.

The S2000 page from the American range brochure for the 2003 season.

Push the S2000's engine start button to the left of the steering wheel, and you'll instantly know you're driving something special. The sensation of this car's race-bred heritage becomes increasingly apparent with each mile as you accelerate, carve through corners and bring it to a stop in stunningly rapid fashion. And it all happens with typical Honda durability and dependability.

S2000 includes: 240-hp, 2.0-liter, 16-valve, DOHC VTEC engine • 6-speed manual transmission • Torque-sensing limited-slip differential • Independent in-wheel double wishbone suspension • Electric Power Steering (EPS) • ABS • Electrically powered soft top w/glass rear window • Air conditioning w/air filtration • Power windows, mirrors and door locks • Cruise control • AM/FM/CD audio system • Leather-trimmed seats, door panels and steering wheel • Integrated roll bars • Digital instrument panel

---

Honda S2000

Innovation aus Tradition.

Im Honda S2000 wurde das Konzept eines klassischen Sportwagens mit modernster Rennsporttechnologie harmonisch vereint.

Die Wurzeln des Honda S2000 liegen bei den legendären Zweisitzern von Honda wie dem Ausnahmefahrzeug Honda S800. Natürlich sind auch die Erfahrungen aus Hondas Engagement in der Formel 1 in den Honda S2000 eingeflossen – also aus über 70 Grand-Prix-Siegen, sechs aufeinander folgenden Siegen in der Konstrukteursweltmeisterschaft und fünf Fahrerweltmeisterschaften. Auf diesen Erfolgen baut der Honda S2000 auf und zeigt zukunftsweisende Leistungen.

Honda hielt bereits den bestehenden Rekord für Saugmotoren, der bei 108 PS lag. Bei der Entwicklung des Honda S2000-Motors war es unser Ziel die höchste spezifische Leistung pro Liter Hubraum bei einem Motor ohne Turbosystem zu erzielen. Dazu war Hondas ganzes Know-how auf dem Gebiet der Hightech-Motoren gefragt. Die Ingenieure entschieden, dass aus Gründen der optimalen Gewichtsverteilung ein extrem leistungsstarker, kompakter und leichter Vierzylindermotor die ideale Lösung darstellen würde.

Um mit einem Motor Schritt zu halten, der seine Spitzenleistung bei 8.300 min⁻¹ entwickelt, mussten zudem neue Materialien, Konstruktionsmethoden und Bauteile entworfen werden. Entstanden ist ein einzigartiges Auto, das seine Fahrer begeistern wird.

THE GIOIRE

As far as the regular cars were concerned, the S2000 and S2000 Type V were basically the same for the domestic 2003 season, with prices carried over, and a catalogue that differed only in the coachwork colour section. But with major changes in the wings, Honda took the opportunity to announce something a bit special to round off the AP-120 run.

Launched on 4 October 2002, the 'Gioire' (named after the Italian for rejoice) was a luxury edition of the S2000, sold in unrestricted numbers. Available at 3,680,000 yen in regular guise or 3,860,000 yen with the Type V specification, the Gioire featured special Royal Navy Blue Pearl or Dark Cardinal Red Pearl paintwork with a gold coachline across the top of the wingline, chrome door mirrors, gold-painted BBS alloys (the same style as the optional items), and a tan and black leather interior. Unique items included quilted leather on the seats, door inserts and centre console, and a two-tone steering wheel. While floormats were classed as part of the package, a colour-coded hardtop was listed as a dealer option, along with a DVD-based navigation system.

The Dark Cardinal Red version of the Gioire special edition.

Below: Cover and a few selected pages from a German catalogue dated January 2003. Sadly, there was far too much untouched, retouched and rehashed photography for the contents to be of any great use, the 1999 image used on the cover being a case in point.

Ein ganz **besonderer** Platz.

The tasteful interior treatment of the Gioire models. The S2000 Type V version had a special two-tone steering wheel in silver and black.

The Royal Navy Blue version of the Gioire in strict S2000 guise. This picture was used as the centrefold in the dedicated Gioire model brochure.

The red car featured on the cover of the eight-page brochure.

A major face-lift

"For its 2004 redesign, Honda engineers [have] elevated the S2000 to a higher class by strengthening the all-round performance, enhancing the interior, and giving the exterior a subtly bolder appearance. The net gain is an S2000 that is simultaneously an improved track car and an improved daily driver."
– US press release, October 2003.

The 2004 MY S2000 was an altogether more aggressive looking beast, with restyled bumper mouldings at both ends and larger alloys filling out the wheelarches.

The Honda S2000 had featured in the world's showrooms for four seasons, so, as far as conventional corporate thinking in the 'Land of the Rising Sun' is concerned, while not being able to justify a full model change (FMC) as a true second generation, with an all-new body, it was certainly due a face-lift (or minor change, aka MC, as they like to call it in Japan). But this is where the story gets confusing, and while it makes an author's life difficult, my habit of looking at all the major outlets rather than a specific one is necessary in this case if we are to get the story straight. Why? Because North America gained a new 2.2-litre engine to go with the cosmetic overhaul, but nowhere else did: other markets retained the 2-litre lump in a fresh package, although Japan would eventually inherit the larger power-unit, too.

More confusion exists over the AP1 and AP2 names. Most people refer to the face-lifted car as the AP2, but, in fact, only the 2.2-litre machines are entitled to this designation – a 2-litre model is an AP1 regardless of the body. And if the S2000 had been named according to engine size, in the same manner as the S500, S600 and S800 before it, why wasn't the S2200 moniker used for the AP2? After all, different names had been applied to cars in specific markets in the past, with the US-spec S30-type Datsun 280Z springing immediately to mind – only smaller-engined 260Zs were sold in Europe. I suppose

Honda had worked hard to create an image for the two-seater, and besides, numbering was no longer the exact science it once was. Take modern Mercedes-Benz and BMW vehicles, for instance. Whatever the reason for keeping the S2000 badge – asking around hasn't brought any meaningful answers to the question – at least the car was still alive and kicking. For that, sports car fans everywhere had to be grateful, whatever engine they had in their particular market ...

THE 2004 CAR IN AMERICA
With the biggest changes taking place in the States, it makes sense to start with the US-spec car. The F22C engine was actually very similar to the F20C unit, with the same basic construction and technical features. The main difference was in the adoption of a longer stroke (90.7mm, against 84.0mm), which increased displacement to 2157cc, and, in conjunction with some fresh camshaft profiles, gave far superior power delivery in the low- to mid-range – a sensible move given American tastes and road conditions, albeit at a marginal cost of top-end sharpness.

In fact, looking at the power and torque curves, their shapes were very similar, it's just that the peak of 240bhp came in 500rpm lower down the rev-range, and significantly more torque (around ten per cent) was

The 2.2-litre F22C engine, readily identified by the champagne-coloured plug cover: the F20C unit retained a black one. Only America had this four-cylinder lump originally, though Japan would adopt it for the 2006 season.

The new 17in alloy wheels, which were the same for all markets, as were the tyres fitted to them.

As can be seen in this picture of a US-spec car, the front-end was transformed via a new bumper moulding and modified light units.

A close-up of the rear combination lamp introduced for the 2004 season.

Detail shot of the latest headlight assembly.

Tail of the 2004 MY car.

fifth (0.94 instead of 0.97) brought the overall difference one per cent lower, while a new sixth (0.76 compared to 0.81 before) made the overall gearing two per cent higher for improved fuel consumption when cruising. In addition, the all-brass synchronisers were changed to a new version using brass with carbon-fibre inserts. These improved feel and reduced mechanical loss, making shifts easier, aided by an uprated clutch mechanism. At the back, the differential casing was strengthened, and the gears within were manufactured in a different way to enhance wear resistance.

With regard to the chassis components, the most obvious change was the adoption of a 17in wheel and tyre combination. The ten-spoke wheels were wider than before, with 7J rims at the front and 8.5J versions at the rear, and shod with 215/45 and 245/40 WR-rated Bridgestone Potenza RE050 tyres. Track dimensions remained the same, however.

Having first reinforced the body in several places for 2004 (with extra metal in the front crossmembers and rear bulkhead, along with a performance bar up front to give roughly a ten per cent improvement in rigidity), with more grip provided by the wider rubber but the ultimate aim of making the car less tricky on the limit, the suspension tuning was completely revised. While the front anti-roll bar was carried over, that at the rear was reduced in diameter to 25.4mm (1.00in) to soften things at the tail-end, and combined with a seven per cent increase in the spring rate up front and a ten per cent decrease at the back. Naturally, the shock absorbers were recalibrated to suit these new settings. With a number of improved suspension bushings, the overhaul was completed by a reduction in the rear toe angle and creating a lower roll centre at the rear to combat bump steer.

The EPS steering system was refined through new software that enhanced linearity, and new mounts for the rack, along with a revised steering ratio to make things less frenetic at the wheel; it now took 2.6 turns to go from lock-to-lock rather than 2.4, at least on US cars, giving the feeling of greater stability. As for the brakes, the brake pad material was changed for improved pedal feel and fade resistance, the master cylinder was tweaked (again, to give the pedal more feel), and the software and hardware controlling the ABS system was modified to reduce weight whilst also increasing efficiency.

Moving on to the styling, the new front and rear

available in the 2500-7000rpm band, only dropping off to levels below those of the 2-litre lump beyond the 8000rpm mark, which is where the new red-line was anyway. In other words, the car was far more suited to everyday traffic – practical, even – yet still a high-revving track tool if the driver felt in the mood to burn some rubber.

Apart from an 11.1:1 compression ratio, all the other leading features regarding the engine were carried over from the F20C. Developing 240bhp at 7800rpm, along with 162lbft of torque at 6500rpm (instead of 153 at 7500, indicating a significant shift in the output curve), amazingly, the F22C was still able to clear the LEV codes, meaning it was exceptionally kind to the environment. With a broader power band that was easier to access, and the throttle travel revised to make it a slightly less delicate instrument, the latest car was kinder to drivers with less experience or big clogs, too.

While an automatic transmission (AT) remained unavailable, the gearing on the 6MT unit was revised. Although the internal ratios were unchanged on first through fourth, a fresh secondary reduction gear (from 1.16 to 1.21) gave the effect of making them four per cent lower. With this new reduction gear ratio, a new cog for

(Continues page 109)

Interior of the 2004 MY car for American shores, including a shot of the updated gauge pack. US-spec cars are easy to spot, incidentally, as they're the only ones amongst the main markets to feature cruise control, and the buttons on the steering wheel are always clearly in view.

S2000

Honda 2004

The majority of the 2004 S2000 catalogue for America. Most of the artwork would be recycled in years to come, some of it even retouched to allow for updates.
(Pages 104 to 107)

Inspiration strikes hard.
The harder the better.

fueled

The S2000 may have four wheels, but it has a one-track mind when it's carving through curves. *Autoweek* magazine summed it up well when they referred to the edgy S2000 as "the ultimate 4-wheeled motorcycle."[1]

One close encounter with the S2000's potential, and you may be left a bit breathless, wondering what inspired such a raw expression of performance. But in creating it, Honda engineers didn't really need to seek inspiration. Because in the world we live in, it keeps finding us. It's in the loud metallic wail of our racing engines, and in the intoxicating aromas of high-octane fuel and hot, sticky rubber pulling at asphalt. We listened. We tuned in. And for 2004, we built an S2000 even more forceful, responsive and refined. More inspired than ever before.

rush

It's not impolite to stare at something truly beautiful. Smooth contours balance sharp lines for a shape that's a touch elegant, yet unapologetic about its hard-edged intentions. For 2004, a more aerodynamic nose features a larger front air intake and high-intensity discharge (HID) headlights. Look closely. Beauty is in the details, like the new center console and cool metallic-finish interior trim. Now climb in, look up at endless sky and forward to an endless road. Complete the picture.

For 2004, the S2000's sporty intentions are punctuated with larger 17-inch alloy wheels shod with low, wide P245/40 R17 rubber in back to get power to pavement, and with P215/45 R17 tires in front for directional control.

If they see you coming or just catch a glimpse of you going, the S2000's new chiseled nose and combination LED taillights will turn more than a few heads. Its freshly sculpted lines speak the language of zip fluently.

applied

The S2000 epitomizes racing heritage applied to the street. Its DNA is that of a pure thoroughbred racer, with a lineage like a road map of Honda engineering milestones. Through thinking that defies conventional limitations, we develop ground-breaking technology that wins races. Those innovations take street-legal form in the fantastically fun-to-drive S2000. Take a trip around your neighborhood, and hear those Formula One genes loud and clear. You may even think about building a grandstand in the driveway.

Honda's latest racing efforts focus on the IRL series, where we will compete with a completely new, normally aspirated V-8 engine.

Honda's revolutionary, V-5 engine-powered RC211V raced to a World Championship in its 2002 debut season.

240
2.2 horsepower liters

S2000 shown in Sebring Silver Metallic

Sometimes, just numbers can tell a thrilling tale. For 2004, we've increased the displacement of the S2000's engine to 2.2 liters with a longer stroke, and increased its compression ratio too. It's still amazingly lightweight and compact, making 240 horsepower and 161 lb.-ft. of torque. Take those forceful figures, factor in some revised overall gear ratios, and the '04 S2000 driver is now treated to an even more exhilarating driving experience. Mere facts and figures can't fully describe seat-of-the-pants fun. But numbers just don't lie. And they can even be poetry in motion.

We redesigned the '04 S2000 instrument panel for even better visibility. As that bold, bright and beautifully flaring digital tach zips toward redline, you get an ever-present lesson in acceleration. And the harder you prod the S2000, the higher you rev that eager engine, the more you realize this car was built to be worked over. It just loves the attention.

Give the irresistibly red start button a push, and you're only scratching the surface of the S2000's similarities to a motorsports machine. Honda racing engineers developed its engine components and systems, carefully honing ultra-lightweight materials to meet exacting tolerances. This use of advanced technology combined with a close attention to precision yields abundant power teamed with remarkable durability. Plus the added convenience of no scheduled tune-ups for 105,000 miles.*

forcefully focused

The S2000's engine is lightweight, and also surprisingly compact considering how much power it puts out. This is achieved with technology like a narrow DOHC design with a space-efficient silent-chain primary drive and gear-driven secondary drive. The geared drive also improves timing accuracy.

Honda's revolutionary variable valve timing and lift electronic control (VTEC*) technology overcomes a longtime limitation of traditional engine design. With VTEC, no compromises have to be made between low- and high-rpm performance. One cam lobe is tuned for low-end torque. Rev higher, and another lobe takes over valve operation for a boost in high-end horsepower. So whatever the engine speed, power and efficiency are always optimized.

*Does not apply to fluid and filter change. See your owner's manual for details.

Heavy is bad. Light is good. It's a simple idea, but it takes some pretty sophisticated thinking to make it a reality. Our engineers used lightweight aluminum alloy to create the S2000's engine block, cylinder head and oil pan. And super-light forged alloy pistons do their business in cylinder liners that are composed of fiber-reinforced metal (FRM), another trick Honda-developed weight-savings feature. These components help form an engine that is free-revving, efficient and amazingly lightweight, yet still strong and durable.

Friction is your foe, but the S2000 slips through its grasp. It has pistons that are shaped with a reduced skirt area for minimal drag between piston and cylinder wall. Less friction means less heat, enabling the engine to operate at higher rpms and to put out more power. The engine also uses a low-friction roller bearing cam follower system, further reducing power losses to friction.

For 2004, the S2000's engine displacement gets a 10% increase, from 2.0 liters to 2.2 liters. And that little bump makes a big difference in the S2000's power characteristics, providing more low-end torque for more thrilling real-world drives. Whether accelerating from a stop or passing at speed, you'll have power on tap across the powerband. Zipping from zero to 60 is always fun, but the best gauges of the S2000's engine improvements aren't clock ticks or skid pads. It's the mega-doses of adrenaline that'll be pumping through your veins.

striking balance

Any racer will tell you. Going fast is more about consistent control than sheer power. For 2004, we refined the S2000's chassis and suspension to help grant its driver complete command when the going gets curvy. The monocoque body and high X-bone frame already had torsional rigidity higher than that of many hard-topped sports cars. For '04, we further increased rigidity with body reinforcements and a new crossmember for super-sharp handling with an even more direct feel. And the gas-pressurized mono-tube shocks, coil springs and rear stabilizer bars are revised for better road-holding in quick corners, as well as improved ride comfort at any speed.

S2000 shown in Rio Yellow Pearl

We positioned the lightweight 2.2-liter powerplant far back in the engine bay, entirely behind the front axle. It's part of our efforts to optimize handling by centralizing the mass of the S2000, creating what our handling-obsessed engineers call a low polar moment of inertia.

When combined with a remarkable power-to-weight ratio and the quick electric power assisted rack-and-pinion steering (EPS), mass centralization helps the S2000 pivot around corners with ease. The EPS system has been recalibrated for '04, for improved response and driver control.

Fully independent double wishbone suspension at all four corners features an in-wheel design for ideal geometry and a low center of gravity for quick weight transfer. For 2004, a lower roll center gives an even more linear response to driver input. And an improved ABS system offers a shorter pedal stroke as well as more progressive pedal feel, and teams with big brake rotors to help slow you down quick.

connect

If you've ever slipped inside a Formula One cockpit, the S2000's interior may feel vaguely familiar. The gauges and controls are prominent and logically placed, creating an intuitive driver interface that's intimate, but also comfortable. High-bolstered leather seats cradle and brace you for quick maneuvers, and the leather-trimmed door panels have been resculpted, offering a bit more elbow room. Your hand finds the shifter while your feet fall naturally on the textured metal pedals, perfectly positioned for quick heel-toe downshifts. Purposeful, yet so refined. Racers should have it so good!

The S2000's power convertible top is easy to drop, and it has a glass rear window, too. The acrylic aero-screen keeps wind buffeting in check. Driver and passenger safety is aided by dual front airbags* (SRS), rollbars and seat belts anchored to the seat, floor and rollbar. And for extra security, the S2000 is guarded by an Immobilizer Theft-Deterrent System.*

S2000 interior shown in Red and Black Leather.

*Please consult an owner's manual for important safety information.

Grab hold of the leather-wrapped aluminum shift knob and snap through the S2000's six gears with firm, short throws. For 2004, slick, tough carbon synchronizers smooth the way, and the overall gear ratios are revised for stronger acceleration in lower gears. Wind it out. Make that 240-horsepower engine sing.

control

Take command of the S2000, and you complete its purpose. Power windows, mirrors and door locks with remote entry ease your access. An easier-to-read instrument panel reports vital information. Stow your gear in the center console bin and larger door pockets. Beverage holders stand by. Set the electronically controlled air conditioning to your ideal zone. Intuitively placed left-hand audio-system controls and steering wheel-mounted cruise control keep you seamlessly connected even while under way. All systems go. Jet pilots shouldn't get to have all the fun.

When the imagined becomes real,
thoughts fade and senses reign.

accessories

Your dealer can help you personalize your new S2000 with a wide selection of Genuine Honda Accessories. And if you have them installed at the time of vehicle purchase, they're covered by the standard Honda 3-year, 36,000-mile limited warranty.[2]

Headrest Speaker System	Ashtray	Front Underbody Spoiler
XM® Satellite Radio[1]	Cargo Net	Trunk Spoiler
Hardtop	Engine Block Heater	Wing Spoiler
Hardtop Storage Rack	Seatback Pocket	Side Strakes
Hardtop Storage Cover	Titanium Shift Knob	Wheel Locks
6-Disc CD Changer	Security System	Vehicle Dust Cover

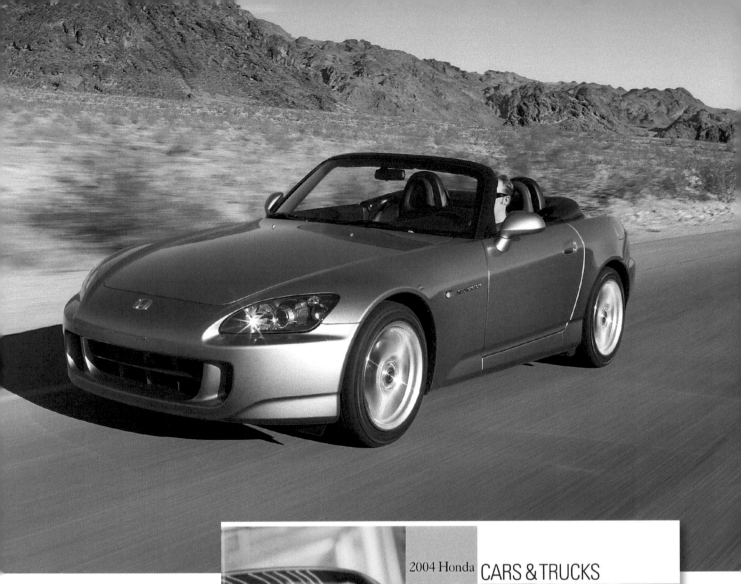

Most testers in America agreed that the 2.2-litre engine was far better suited to US roads and driving styles than the original F20C unit had been.

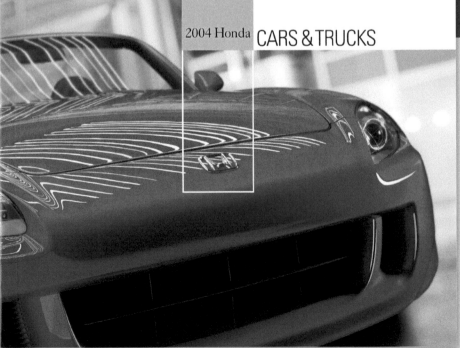

2004 Honda CARS & TRUCKS

A red S2000 gracing the cover of the US range brochure for the 2004 season.

bumper mouldings gave the S2000 a more powerful look, along with a five per cent improvement in the car's Cd value, although the body dimensions were unchanged. By moving the faux brake cooling ducts closer to the centre of the vehicle, it gave the impression of a larger intake, while the feature lines added interest at the sides of the nose panel. The transformation was completed via new headlights, which had a dynamic appearance thanks to a fresh configuration within the clear lens. The main beam design was much the same, but the HID unit for low beam was more stylish, and extended to form a mount for the amber reflector. The circular indicator and sidelight units were separated and placed on the outboard edge of the projector light casing.

The face-lifted model had only just been launched, but it didn't stop King Motorsports (Mugen's official distributor for the USA) having a fully modified car ready for the 2003 SEMA Show, which opened in November.

Around the back, the new bolder look was much in evidence, with the revised bumper moulding being much stronger in appearance. Gone was the central character line, dropped in favour of an extended skirt-cum-exhaust surround that gave the impression of the car sitting lower, even though it wasn't in reality. The folds in the doors were continued down the sides of the new bumper section, helping to highlight the latest wheel design. A darkened, crisper tail-light assembly was also part of the makeover (following a similar styling theme as the headlights, with the extensive use of LED lamps allowing the brake lights to move inside an outer tail-light ring), along with beefier oval-shaped chrome tailpipe finishers.

The interior was also freshened up, with increased space and improved storage. In front of the driver, there was a new 'H' logo badge on the horn pad, a 'Cancel' button added to the cruise control switches below it, and revised dashboard graphics, with the tachometer read-out travel shortened and the fresh coolant temperature and fuel gauges now off to the right. There was another

button at the base of the instrument panel for the digital clock, which at last found its way into the gauge pack, sitting between the speedometer and odometer.

Further items aimed at brightening up the interior were adopted, including an embossed aluminium-style audio cover (with a matching finish on the console lid immediately aft of the gearbox, which now had a one-touch release and contained two cup holders), silver dressing pieces for the headrest backs, and a fresh gearknob, albeit similar to the 2003 type, just with a more rounded top. Ironically, the switchgear panel inlays on each side of the steering wheel were blacked out (albeit with a gloss finish) in a bid to balance the latest shiny bits. At the same time, the door trim was restyled to provide a fraction more room for folks to manoeuvre, as well as better storage in the lower pocket, and the door-mounted tweeters were now housed behind more modest covers.

On the face of it, very little had changed on the colour and trim charts for US buyers, but the red trim was now a

An S2000 taking centre stage on the Honda stand at the San Jose Show, January 2004. (Courtesy Ken Hoyle)

two-tone affair, using a black base with red inlays on the seats and doors. Black was still all-black, and blue was all-blue, although the tan option was a mixture, being mainly tan, but using a black console and door casings to provide some contrast.

With a new EPA rating of 20/25, the 1288kg (2835lb) 2004 model S2000 was listed at $32,800. This compares with a starting price of $13,010 for the Civic range and a $15,900 entry price for the Accords, although the Accord V6 coupé commanded as much as $28,500. More importantly, perhaps, at one end, the Mazda MX-5 Miata cost around $22,000 in its cheapest guise, while at the other, the Porsche Boxster would have set a potential buyer back at least $42,600. Both rivals would be seen as fresh generation models soon after, of course.

Standard features included a power soft top, HID headlights, 17in alloy wheels, variable-ratio power-assisted steering, a limited-slip differential, ABS braking, power mirrors, power windows, air-conditioning, a windblocker device, remote control central locking (with separate boot release), dual airbags, cruise control, leather seats, a leather-trimmed steering wheel and gearknob, storage boxes and dual cup holders, a 30W CD/radio, 12V power socket, immobiliser, and floormats. Headrest speakers (two per seat) were a new option, augmenting the four that came as part of the stock

S2000 spec, along with a $550 XM satellite radio package. One could also specify a hardtop and/or a rear spoiler.

Rexx Taylor tried the new car for the San Francisco Chronicle, and concluded: "The Honda S2000 is a pleasant enough street car, a very lively roadster and a competent track car. It's not really suited for casual transportation, but it is a true sports car and one for the purists. Each ride is an invigorating experience." This, of course, was part of the reason why the S2000 kept on being elected to Car & Driver's '10 Best' year after year.

Having called the new model a "more satisfying real-world performer" in an earlier article, Motor Trend conducted an interesting three-way test involving the face-lifted S2000, the Nissan 350Z and Mazda RX-8 to find what makes a modern sports car, with instrumented tests balanced by subjective ratings. With a 0-60 time of 5.8 seconds, and the standing-quarter mark dismissed 8.4 seconds later, the Honda was in the middle of the bunch, with the Z fastest. The S2000 gave the best skidpan results, with 0.9g, but lost this advantage in the braking distance tests. That said, the car shone in the figure-of-eight run that took in a combination of acceleration, handling and braking. This was not enough to give the Honda the nod, though: "Despite, or perhaps because of, its new-found 'civilisation' programme

A final shot from the 2004 US press pack, which is just too attractive to leave out. Note the North American specification cars still retained a black windscreen frame rather than the colour-keyed one adopted elsewhere.

and a slight weight gain, the 2004 S2000 produces performance numbers only marginally diminished from what they used to be. Honda figures giving up a small measure of performance for a noticeably less taxing experience will drive more buyers. What once felt like a club racer with a licence plate has been brought only a bit closer to the sweet spot of what most people would consider an acceptable daily driver. However, driving all three of our competitors back-to-back, the S2000's comfort-be-damned mission continues to shine through. If you currently own a motorcycle and are looking to come out of the cold, this is the perfect car."

THE 'AP2' IN JAPAN
Firstly, we need to clarify the subtitle. The face-lifted car of 2004 was not an AP2 as far as the domestic market

was concerned – it was a variation of the AP1 series (the AP1-130 in this case) due to the continued use of the 2-litre engine, and it's the powerplant that dictates the chassis code, rather than the appearance of the body. That doesn't stop enthusiasts using the term loosely, but one has to be aware of the correct definition at least.

Anyway, the 2003 Tokyo Show (which opened at Makuhari Messe at the end of October) held a lot of interest for Honda fans, as the HSC concept gave a hint of what the next NSX generation might look like, and, perhaps more importantly, the opportunity was taken to launch the latest incarnation of the S2000. Appointed as Honda's latest President in June that year, Takeo Fukui (a man equally at home talking to workers on the factory floor as we has strapped into the cockpit of an F1 car, or sitting astride a racing motorcycle) was in his element.

Selected pages from the Japanese catalogue dated October 2003, including the one showing the latest Modulo bodykit. The cover was given a silver metallic look to match the interior upgrades.
(Pages 112 to 115)

ドアセンターパード、ショルダー部の空間が広がり、村づちまわり周辺がゆったりしたネジション環境
輪からヘッドライトに、とはノーズに、というスポーツカーの基本が貫かれている

シルバーのメタリーナな質かが、さらかしここに譲りトライバーズ空間
ステアリングホイールやオーシコンプーンにも新たに加えられ、本来プラークのたくわしきが調境を見せる

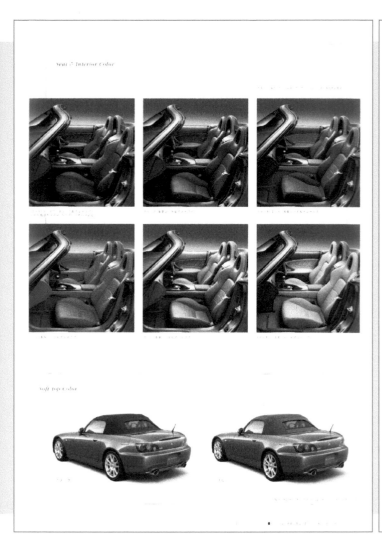

スポーツカードライブに応える、
Honda・DVDナビゲーションシステム。

データベースにDVD-ROMを採用したHonda・DVDナビゲーションシステム
豊富な情報量に加え、スクロール、現在、ルート探索の高速
表示スケールは、10m縮尺の市街地図表示、表示スタイルは
3Dシステムワイド、な、各テナント施設表示、レーン情報表示機能
高速道路分岐点拡大機能、などバリエーションも豊か。

また、経路探索、到着予定時間、音声ガイドなどの各種機能も充実
もちろん、渋滞などとの情報をリアルタイムに表示する
VICS・道路交通情報通信システム、双方向通信機能をもち
インターナビシステムにも対応している。また、TV放送が楽しめる
TVチューナーユニッ ～ ～ ～ ～ ～ 、も用意されている。

internavi

■ ～ ～ ～ ～ ～

軽量アルミ製・低重心のエアロダイナミクスデザイン
四季は、紫外線保護を考慮、デザインのうえにコンセプトルーフを採用
クーペを思わせる、スタイリッシュなフォルムインテリア
脊椎は1点ロック不動式で、ルーフを名有しシート に身を沈むのも。
タイトな、一快感がドライバーを温かく包む

Officially on sale at Verno dealers from 17 October, a few days before the show, the face-lifted S2000 continued to employ the 250PS F20C engine, albeit in a stronger bodyshell, and mated to an improved 6MT transmission with carbon-fibre synchros to give slicker shifts. For the record, JDM gear ratios were carried over in full, including the 1.16 secondary reduction ratio of old.

Naturally, though, the styling changes found on the US cars were adopted for the domestic vehicles, too, with new bumper mouldings front and rear, updated lights that were close to standardised across all markets (at least in appearance), and big bore oval tailpipes. The 17in alloys were also the same as those found in the States, as well as the WR-rated tyres they were shod with. Beyond the wheels, new brake pads were employed to reduce fade, and the suspension mods outlined earlier helped tame the handling. Japanese cars also adopted the 2.6 turns lock-to-lock steering ratio used in America at this time

on the strict S2000; the Type V model continued with its ultra-fast 1.4 turns lock-to-lock setup.

The interior was also brought up-to-date, with the latest steering wheel boss (the Type V inherited the two-tone steering wheel from Gioire, by the way), and a revised gauge pack visible behind it. The metallic accents added to the centre console, audio lid and headrest backs also put in an appearance, along with the revised gearknob and door furniture. All-red leather and black cloth trim options were listed in Japan, and with the new tan interior and fresh paintwork choices (plus two soft top hues, of course), buyers were given an amazing 156 variations to mull over.

3,500,000 yen was the asking price for a strict 2004 MY S2000, while the Type V commanded 200,000 yen more. Premium paint added 200,000 yen, leather trim 100,000 yen, and a DVD-based navigation system 220,000 yen.

Incidentally, there was a brief period when the

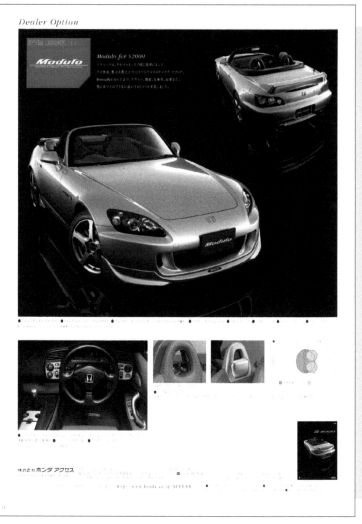

JAPANESE (JDM) LATE AP1 & AP2 COLOUR AND TRIM OPTIONS

This sidebar charts the changes in the coachwork colour and interior trim for the JDM S2000, with the date being the month in which sales of updated vehicles began.

October 2003: Colour palette revised to include Silverstone Metallic, Sebring Silver Metallic, Moon Rock Metallic, Berlina Black, New Formula Red, Royal Navy Blue Pearl, Nürburgring Blue Metallic, New Indy Yellow Pearl and Grand Prix White as regular paint shades, with Platinum White Pearl, Monza Red Pearl, Lime Green Metallic, and New Imola Orange Pearl offered as additional 'Premium' choices. Trim came in black vinyl with a cloth insert, with black, red, red/black, blue or light tan leather as an option. Hood available in black or blue.

November 2005: Bermuda Blue Pearl and Deep Burgundy Metallic added as regular paint shades, but only Platinum White Pearl and New Imola Orange Pearl now offered as additional 'Premium' choices. Trim colours changed, now coming in black vinyl with a cloth insert, with black, red, brown or blue leather as an option.

October 2007: Colour palette revised to include Synchro Silver Metallic, Moon Rock Metallic, Berlina Black, New Formula Red, Bermuda Blue Pearl, New Indy Yellow Pearl and Grand Prix White as regular paint shades, with Apex Blue Pearl for the Type S only (replaces Bermuda Blue Pearl on that model); Platinum White Pearl and Premium Sunset Mauve Pearl offered as additional 'Premium' choices. The blue leather trim option was dropped, while the Type S was sold with black/yellow cloth trim as standard, with black, red or brown leather as an option. Hood still available in black or blue.

One of the pictures from the 2004 Geneva Show press pack, showing a left-hand drive car for mainland Europe. All European cars (including UK models) gained a small 'Honda' plaque above the 'S2000' example on the front wings at this time, although, strangely, these chrome badges were not adopted elsewhere.

AP1-135 designation was used (in the early part of spring 2004), which is also when the LA chassis code changed to an ABA one. This was in recognition of the S2000 complying with the forthcoming 2005 JDM emission codes, thanks to an improved air-fuel ratio sensor and fuel injector.

It should be noted that the specialist part of the Takanezawa Plant looking after NSX and S2000 production closed on 3 April 2004. This was not the end of the story, though, as production moved to Honda's Suzuka factory (close to the Grand Prix circuit) instead, prompting a fresh AP1-200 code for the S2000. The 'Small Volume Speciality Cars' facilities didn't go to waste, though, as the innovative FCX fuel cell-powered model was built in Tochigi from mid-2008.

Time was definitely running out for the NSX, but, for the time being at least, unlike so many of its contemporaries, the mid-engined Honda survived. However, not long after the move to Suzuka, a press release stated that NSX production would come to a halt at the end of 2005, and, while prototypes of its replacement were spotted, the Lehman Shock would prove to be the final nail in the coffin for the supercar.

OTHER MARKETS FOR 2004

Introduced at the Geneva Show, Britain duly launched the face-lifted S2000 in April 2004, with the strict model costing £26,513 and the GT (which came with a detachable hardtop as part of the package), £27,513 – both up a modest £513 on the earlier version. The European cars inherited all the modifications and styling revisions introduced in Japan (as well as colour-keyed headlight washer housings, rather than black ones, and small 'Honda' badges finding their way onto the front wings), prompting many to call this an AP2 model, although it isn't, because the free-revving F20C engine was retained, as it was for the home market. There's no doubt, though, that it looks different to the 2003 cars, and the moniker is useful enough to mark the face-lift. After all, European vehicles would keep the 2-litre powerplant through to the end of S2000 production, so there's little chance of getting them mixed up.

Australians were able to buy the new model from March 2004, priced at $74,590, as before, and retaining the 2-litre lump mated up to a six-speed manual transmission. Coachwork colours were also carried over, with New Formula Red, Berlina Black, Grand Prix White,

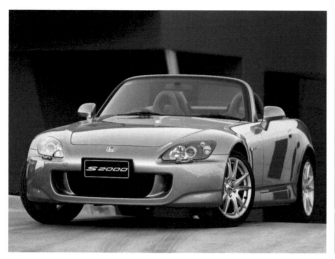

Front and tail views of the Australian S2000 from 2004, which differed from the UK model in not having 'Honda' badges on the front wings, or a rear foglight. The alloy wheels were the same as those fitted in Japan, America and Europe, though.

Silverstone Metallic, Indy Yellow Pearl, Nürburgring Blue Metallic, and Monte Carlo Blue shades available.

THE 2005 SEASON

According to American press releases from the time, the only change for 2005 was in the pricing – even the colour charts were carried over. Quoting the blurb, the $32,950 (rising to $33,150 in the spring of 2005) S2000 "symbolises the best of Honda's performance engineering. More than just fun to drive, the S2000 puts

The cockpit of the same car.

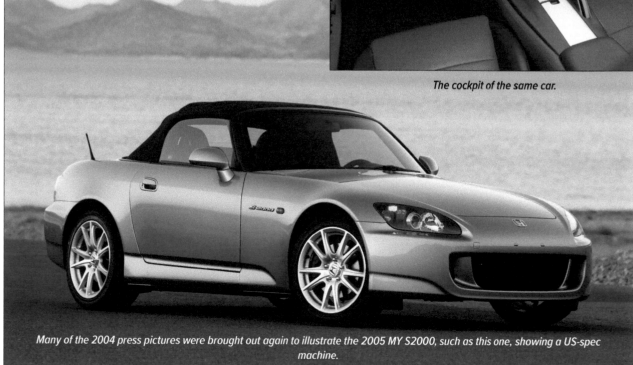

Many of the 2004 press pictures were brought out again to illustrate the 2005 MY S2000, such as this one, showing a US-spec machine.

Cover from the 2005 S2000 catalogue for America. The contents were very similar to those seen in the 2004 version.

Honda's advanced racing technologies into a car that can be driven every day."

The specifications were carried over in Japan and

NORTH AMERICAN VIN CODES

The VIN codes, or chassis numbers if you like, consist of 17 digits. The first three ('JHM') denote Honda, while the next three are 'AP1' for 2-litre cars, and 'AP2' for models with the 2.2-litre engine. The seventh digit is for the body type, with a '1' to depict a two-door convertible with a 6MT gearbox, followed by either a '4' for regular S2000s or a '2' for the CR grade. Next is a check digit, from '0' to '9' inclusive, plus 'X' being used. The tenth is a model year (MY) code, with 'Y' for 2000, '1' for 2001, '2' for 2002, and so on, until '9' for 2009. This is followed by a factory code, with 'T' for Tochigi (up to and including 2004), and 'S' for Suzuka (2004 and onwards). The final six numbers start on 000001 for US cars, and 800001 for Canadian machines.

Europe, too. In Britain, the strict S2000 was listed at £26,600 going into the 2005 season, against £27,600 for the GT grade. To put this into perspective, NSX prices started at £61,100, while the Jazz (or Fit) was available from £8600; the top Mazda MX-5 was £18,000 at the time.

Notwithstanding, Robin Roberts noted in the motoring section of the *Coventry Evening Telegraph*: "Honda always had a good car trying to get out of the cushy confines of the S2000 chassis, and it has now made it more of a driver's car than ever ... The S2000 really is an exceptionally fine, modern two-seater sports car."

Prices increased by £730 in the spring of 2005, and were rounded off to £26,800 and £27,800 at the end of the year. Australian enthusiasts were luckier, for the 2005 model was listed at $72,590 (a reduction of $2000 on the previous season's pricing), although Aussie sales were down to a trickle by now ...

In the background, things began to come together in the company's F1 programme during 2004, and, after a disappointing couple of years, Honda clinched yet

A 2005-registered S2000 on British roads, and the interior of the same car. Interestingly, European cars had the heated rear window switch moved to the centre console earlier than other markets – moved there from the 2004 season, as it happens, with heated mirrors also activated by the same switch. It was generally only the rear foglight switch left behind the steering wheel.

A domestic car fitted with a Mugen carbon-fibre 'aero bonnet,' a glass-fibre 'front wing,' and adjustable carbon-fibre rear spoiler, as well as the company's MF10 alloy wheels.

another Indycar title, beating Toyota and Chevrolet by quite some margin. Tony Kanaan won the drivers' crown in a Dallara-Honda, followed home by Dan Wheldon in a similar machine.

With Jordan having switched to Ford power a couple of seasons earlier, the good results that allowed the BAR-Honda equipe to claim second place in the 2004 F1 series encouraged Honda to take a large stake in the team in time for the 2005 season, but the races that followed were far from brilliant. Nonetheless, Honda persisted and bought the remaining shares in the outfit to create the Honda Racing F1 Team in readiness for 2006. The Super Aguri F1 team sprang up at the same time, but lasted only three seasons, with a sixth place being the best it could muster during that period. Honda's own efforts were not suitably rewarded either, and the company pulled out of the Formula One game at the end of 2008, albeit spawning the highly-successful Brawn GP team as a consequence.

Britain's Dan Wheldon romped home with the 2005 Indycar title, driving an Andretti Green Racing Dallara-Honda. However, following the withdrawal of Toyota and Chevrolet from the Indycar scene, Honda became the sole engine supplier for all teams for several years from 2006 onwards, so naturally picked up the honours, whoever was driving!

The twilight years

And so we approach the end of the story, where things get even more convoluted with Japan adopting the full AP2 specification for the 2006 season, and all markets receiving a flurry of upgrades and special editions to allow the S2000 to go out with a bang ...

The domestic car was the one that received the most changes for 2006, so we shall begin with that model. Sales started on 25 November, but the updated S2000 had already been aired at the 39th Tokyo Show a month before, lining up alongside the elegant Sports 4 and FCX concepts, as well as a selection of Honda's racing machinery.

The biggest change for the 2006 Model Year home market S2000 was adoption of the 2.2-litre F22C engine. Naturally, this unit was basically the same as the one already in use in the States, with the familiar 2157cc and 11.1:1 c/r providing 242PS in the catalogues. New for all cars, though, was a computerised drive-by-wire (DBW) throttle system, allowing Honda to

eliminate the traditional cable and tidy up other related components at the same time. Interestingly, the VSA feature (more on which later) was not applied to JDM models.

To match the 2.2-litre powerplant, gearing was changed to the US AP2-spec on the latest Japanese cars, although was carried over on the 2-litre cars still sold in Europe and the Antipodes (while the part number on the secondary shaft was different on 2004 cars, the ratio was retained, along with those on the internal cogs and final-drive – something much easier to check). As such, like the vehicles shipped to America, JDM cars

The face-lifted S2000 on display at the 2005 Tokyo Motor Show, seen here in Type V guise. These latest JDM models carried the AP2-100 internal designation.

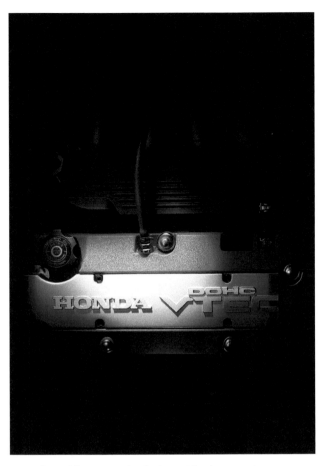

Something new under the bonnet for Japanese buyers.

handbrake, a subtly darker audio lid, and an outside temperature read-out added next to the clock in the dash; the security system was also improved with the addition of an alarm (not previously part of the JDM package).

On sale in Japan from 25 November 2005, the strict 2.2-litre S2000 was listed at 3,780,000 yen including tax (Japan's VAT had stood at five per cent since 1997), with the S2000 Type V commanding 3,990,000 yen. Premium paint cost 210,000 yen, leather trim 105,000 yen, and a DVD navigation system was available for 231,000 yen. Having had monthly sales expectations in the 300s, Honda was now aiming to shift 100 cars a month through its domestic dealer network.

In the background, the former Primo, Clio and Verno sales channels merged to become 'Honda Cars' dealers in March 2006. It made sense, as most of the Japanese car sales organisations have streamlined their businesses in recent years, and several lines were shared amongst them, anyway. Domestic sales of home-produced machines had hit the 5,000,000 mark in 1990, but were closer to 4,000,000 by the end of the decade. While they would rise again, with 4,750,000 Japanese-made vehicles finding new homes in 2005 (only 280,000 import cars were sold in the same year – well under half of Honda's JDM sales), smaller models and minivans accounted for most of that figure, and profits were generally tighter as manufacturers continued to compete via low pricing in these segments.

THE US MARKET FOR 2006

Following the JDM lead, and on sale from the end of October 2005, the 2006 MY S2000 inherited a lot of new features in the States – some cosmetic, some more meaningful. Of course, the 2.2-litre F22C engine was already in place in America, although it was now rated at 237bhp at 7800rpm (due simply to a revised way of measuring SAE net output), and delivered 162lbft at 6800rpm, meaning peak torque came in 300rpm higher than before. In the process of this change, brought about by a multitude of minor tweaks aimed at simplifying production (so care needs to be taken when ordering replacement parts for cars of this period), and allowing the new DBW system to work effectively, as well as modifications to the exhaust system (including deletion of the old air pump setup), the EPA rating returned to its former 20/26 figure, while the latest

now came with 0.94 and 0.76 ratios on fifth and sixth, and a 1.21 secondary reduction gear, while those for European and Australasian markets had figures of 0.97, 0.81 and 1.16 for the same slots on the spec sheet. First through fourth and final-drive ratios were still the same for all markets.

While there were no bodywork revisions, other than changes in the colour palette, the 2006 MY cars were treated to new, albeit similar, ten-spoke aluminium alloy wheels, with the same rim and tyre sizes as before. Inside, there were fresh trim colours, new seats with a stronger frame and revised headrests (now slab-shaped instead of hooped, although the rest of the seat design was similar to the earlier versions), black door inlays for all trim options (it should be noted, though, that some export markets, such as America and Europe, retained a two-tone inlay and two-tone seats on red trim for 2006 and 2007), a restyled steering wheel boss, a much darker lid and dressing piece to the side of the

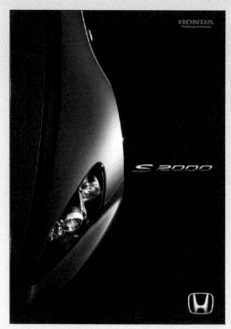

Selected images from the domestic catalogue, dated November 2005. Note the different interior options. (continues overleaf)

シート表皮は革シボやパンチングに手を加え、上質感と繊細さを兼ね備えた仕上がりとしている。
新たなレースバックデザインとあいまってドライバーをタイトに包み込む。

よりスポーティで精悍さを強調したステアリングがひときわ目を引くドライバーズ空間。
シルバーメタリックとブラックを基調とする硬質なデザインポリシーが、インテリア全体との統一感を醸し出す。

Seat & Interior Color

Soft-Top Color

Dealer Option

Modulo
Honda Custom Performance

Interior of the regular S2000 for Japan's 2006 season, exposed properly thanks to the door being removed for photography purposes.

Dashboard details of the S2000 Type V for 2006. Note the special steering wheel and the lack of a third switch aft of the gearbox.

'LEV 2' Californian emissions codes were passed with relative ease.

In addition to the DBW setup, US buyers were also given Vehicle Stability Assist (VSA) and the uprated braking system that came with it. To quote the press release: "Working in concert with the drive-by-wire system, VSA continuously monitors yaw rate, steering input, throttle input and braking pressure to determine if the car is following its driver's intended path, and can independently coordinate each of the disc brakes through the four-channel ABS system, along with the throttle, to enhance stability. While this serves to effectively enhance driver control during acceleration, braking and cornering, the system can be disabled with the touch of a button when conditions warrant it. To help provide optimum stopping power, the braking system also features Electronic Brake Distribution (EBD) and Brake Assist (BA)."

The VSA switch took the place previously occupied by the rear screen heater controls, by the way, with the latter now located next to the roof and hazard warning

(Continues page 128)

Two things are always guaranteed at the Auto Salon – plenty of glamour, and plenty of carbon-fibre ...

Opposite and below: The 2006 US catalogue was virtually the same as the 2005 one, with a new cover and a lot of retouched photography, including new wheels for the side view of the silver car in the early pages. The power figure was adjusted from 240 to 237bhp, and there were new interior shots, but otherwise, one was hard-pushed to find the differences.

connect

If you've ever slipped inside a Formula One cockpit, the S2000's interior may feel vaguely familiar. The gauges and controls are prominent and logically placed, creating an intuitive driver interface that's intimate, yet comfortable. The newly redesigned high-bolstered perforated leather seats cradle and brace you for quick maneuvers, while the powerful audio system with speakers in the roll bars provides the ideal soundtrack for your road adventure. To help keep you an informed driver, an exterior temperature indicator has been fitted to the instrument panel. Think of it as road telemetry.

S2000 interior shown in Black Leather.

06 Honda

S2000

Your one-touch connection to 50 years of checkered flags.

The Honda S2000 wasn't just "inspired" by racing. It was developed on the high-speed straightaways, breathtaking sweepers and tight hairpins of Suzuka, site of the Japanese Grand Prix. By engineers who have worked to create Honda's extraordinary heritage of success in motorsports. Settle into the cockpit, run it up through the gears and probe the cornering limits—you'll have no problem discovering this amazing machine's true genetic code. The S2000 is the link between world-beating performance—and you.

The power convertible top is easy to drop, and it has a glass rear window, too. The acrylic aero screen keeps wind buffeting in check. Driver and passenger safety is aided by dual front airbags* (SRS), roll bars and seat belts anchored to the seat, floor and roll bar. And for extra security, there's an Immobilizer Theft-Deterrent System.

*Honda reminds you and your passengers to always buckle up.

S 2000

Cover of the contemporary eight-page Mugen catalogue, along with a shot of the engine bay of a Mugen-tuned S2000 photographed at the 2006 Tokyo Auto Salon.

switches. A computerised maintenance monitor was also new, allowing Honda to extend its regular three-year warranty to five years on powertrain components, as were the latest alloy wheels (the same design as the JDM ones, with more even spacing on the spokes than the 2004-2005 version) and daytime running lights (DRL).

Other minor differences included the addition of an outside temperature gauge, headrest speakers built into the roll-over bar (two in each to give an eight-speaker

SPECIFICATIONS

The leading specifications for the late models, with the home market (JDM) base car shown as the reference vehicle. Significant differences between grades and export models, as well as running changes, are noted against each entry. Special editions are covered within the text.

Model

Code	LA-AP1 or ABA-AP1 (F20C engine), or ABA-AP2 (F22C engine)
Type	Two-seater open car with a power-operated convertible soft top. Steel unit construction body

Engine #1

Code	F20C (for Japan and ROW)
Mounting	Front, longitudinal
Cylinders	Four, water-cooled in two-piece cast aluminium alloy block with FRM cylinder liners
Head	Cast aluminium alloy, with dohc and four valves per cylinder, plus a VTEC variable valve timing mechanism
Capacity	1997cc
Bore & stroke	87.0mm x 84.0mm
Compression ratio	11.7:1 (11.0:1 for ROW)
Fuel delivery	Electronic fuel-injection (PGM-FI)
Ignition	12V electronic, distributorless, with separate coils
Power @ rpm	250PS @ 8300 (240bhp for ROW)
Torque @ rpm	160lbft @ 7500 (153lbft for ROW)

Engine #2

Code	F22C (for USA, and later Japan)
Mounting	Front, longitudinal
Cylinders	Four, water-cooled in two-piece cast aluminium alloy block with FRM cylinder liners
Head	Cast aluminium alloy, with dohc and four valves per cylinder, plus a VTEC variable valve timing mechanism
Capacity	2157cc
Bore & stroke	87.0mm x 90.7mm
Compression ratio	11.1:1
Fuel delivery	Electronic fuel-injection (PGM-FI)
Ignition	12V electronic, distributorless, with separate coils
Power @ rpm	242PS @ 7800 (240bhp, later officially 237bhp for USA)
Torque @ rpm	162lbft @ 6500-7500

Transmission

Gearbox type	Six-speed manual
Clutch	Single dry plate
Internal ratios	3.13, 2.04, 1.48, 1.16, 0.97 and 0.81 with F20C engine, or 3.13, 2.04, 1.48, 1.16, 0.94 and 0.76 with F22C engine
Reverse gear	2.80
Final-drive	4.10:1
Driven wheels	Rear, with limited-slip differential

Chassis

Front suspension	Independent, via double-wishbones, coil springs, and gas-filled tubular shock absorbers. Anti-roll bar 26.5mm (1.04in), later 27.2mm (1.07in); 28.6mm (1.12in) on CR and Type S grades
Rear suspension	Independent, via double-wishbones, coil springs, and gas-filled tubular shock absorbers. Anti-roll bar 25.4mm (1.00in); 26.5mm (1.04in) on CR and Type S grades
Front brakes	300mm (11.8in) diameter ventilated discs, single-pot calipers, with anti-lock system (ABS)
Rear brakes	282mm (11.1in) solid discs, single-pot calipers, with anti-lock system (ABS). Mechanical handbrake mechanism included
Front wheels	Alloys, 7J x 17
Front tyres	215/45 WR17
Rear wheels	Alloys, 8.5J x 17
Rear tyres	245/40 WR17 (255/40 WR17 for CR grade)
Steering	Rack-and-pinion with EPS electrical power assistance
Lock-to-lock	2.6 turns, or 1.4 with VGS system; 2.4 for CR grade

Dimensions

Wheelbase	2400mm (94.5in)
Overall length	4135mm (162.8in), or officially 4120mm (162.2in) for USA
Overall height	1285mm (50.6in)
Body width	1750mm (68.9in)
Front track	1470mm (57.9in)
Rear track	1510mm (59.4in)
Ground clearance	130mm (5.1in)
Fuel capacity	50 litres (11 Imperial gallons)
Typical weight	1240kg (2728lb), or 1260kg (2772lb) with VGS system and F20C engine; 1250kg (2750lb), 1270kg (2794lb) with VGS system and F22C engine, or 1260kg (2772lb) for Type S with F22C engine; 1288kg (2835lb) for USA and ROW, with minimum of 1257kg (2765lb) for CR grade

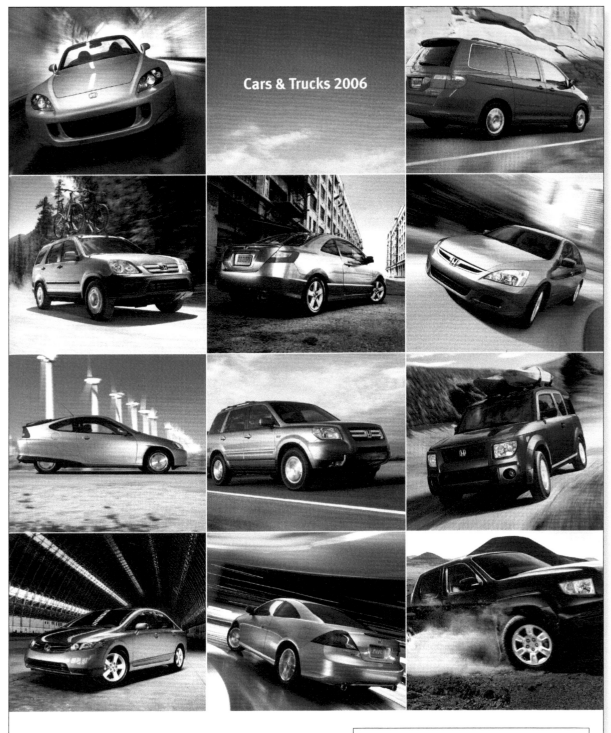

Cars & Trucks 2006

HONDA

Cover from the Canadian Honda range brochure for 2006, showing (left to right, top to bottom) the S2000, Odyssey, CR-V, Civic coupé, Accord sedan, Insight, Pilot, Element, Civic sedan, Accord coupé and Ridgeline models.

S2000

Move both heaven and earth. Simultaneously. By its very nature, by the very design of its sleek monocoque body, the S2000 puts everything behind you. Work. Worries. And, of course, traffic. The awe-inspiring 2.2-litre, 237-hp engine operates 162 lbs-ft of torque. Close ratio gears, 17-inch alloy wheels and a phenomenal power-to-weight ratio all collaborate to make the most of every drive. Now, specs alone can't fully portray on-the-pavement fun. But numbers don't lie, and the numbers say this is a car you're going to want to hit the road in.

Racing heritage is as much a part of the S2000 as you are. Strap yourself in. And take note: any similarities between the cockpit of an F1 race car and the S2000 cockpit that envelops you are intentional. The newly designed high-bolstered perforated leather seats are constructed to cradle and brace you for lightning-fast manoeuvres.

The gauges and controls are prominent and logically placed, creating an intuitive driver interface that is intimate, yet comfortable. Just thinking about it is enough to stir your red blood cells into a frenzy. Great style, great performance and great handling.

Familiar artwork from the Canadian 2006 range brochure, which was rolled out yet again with only slight changes for 2007.

system), refinements to the SRS system (with a passenger airbag cut-off switch added between the vents above the audio lid), and the revised seats, console colouring and steering wheel adopted in Japan. Fresh paint options were combined with a new trim situation: black trim was still all-black, blue trim was now blue seats only, and red trim was a continuation of the 2005 pattern (albeit with a black headrest area) as far as the United States was concerned.

The 2006 S2000, some 9kg (20lb) heavier than before, was priced at $34,050 (a $900 increase), with shipping adding another $550. While the new NC-type Mazda MX-5 was available from $21,435 in basic guise, this compared favourably with the latest incarnations of German machinery such as the $45,000 Porsche Boxster and $46,250 Mercedes-Benz SLK350.

OTHER MARKETS FOR 2006

Naturally, the updated car filtered through to Europe and the Antipodes in due course, albeit still sporting an AP1 designation due to continued use of the 2-litre engine. Trim generally followed the American pattern, with red being a two-tone black and red affair, as before, plus the addition of brown leather in some markets. Germany was a good example, matching Ascari Red, Berlina Black, Deep Burgundy Metallic, Silverstone Metallic, Moon Rock Metallic, Nürburgring Blue Metallic, Bermuda Blue Metallic and New Indy Yellow Pearl paintwork with black, red, blue or brown leather trim, plus either a black or blue soft top (the latter available only with Nürburgring Blue coachwork). Sales in Germany were falling quickly, however, with only 286 S2000s sold there in 2004, 229 in 2005, and 211 in 2006. Ultimately, annual sales would

Various views of the German-spec car for 2006.

fall to 149 in 2007 before dropping off again to 94, then 64 to give a grand total of 4542 cars sold in Germany over the entire production run.

Whilst standard in mainland Europe, VSA was a £300 option in the UK, where the S2000 was now priced at £27,295 in regular guise and £27,845 in GT form. The respected *Car* magazine posed the question many of us wanted to ask: "Aren't electronic driver aids missing

One of the Honda UK press cars: its picture was used in the Car article mentioned below.

the point of an out-and-out sports car like the S2000?" The article continued: "Slightly yes. The Honda has a beautifully balanced chassis for most people's purposes. Around the fast sweeps of Castle Combe circuit, it felt perfectly settled. Through fast corners the rear has a tendency to wander around slightly but once you're accustomed to it, that's of little concern and hardly ever triggers the VSA. The only time the vast majority would ever need VSA would be on a wet road when the rear end could get a bit lively."

In Australia, while the $72,590 sticker price was carried over, Bermuda Blue replaced Monte Carlo Blue to join the existing New Formula Red, Berlina Black, Grand Prix White, Indy Yellow Pearl, Silverstone Metallic and Nürburgring Blue Metallic hues, while trim followed the JDM pattern, so red upholstery, for instance, was a full

Opposite and above: Useful detail and bodywork option pages from the German catalogue dated March 2006.

red seat matched with all-black door casings and console mouldings.

THE 2007 MODEL YEAR

There were no changes in Japan for 2007, with even the coachwork and trim hues carried over. Americans did at least get some different colour schemes to choose from, with white paintwork now matched up with two-tone red and black trim, although a couple of paint shades were lost along the way. Interestingly, the 2.2-litre US-spec cars continued to sport a black windscreen surround – something other markets had dropped long ago in favour of a colour-keyed frame. The 2007 S2000 was priced at $34,250, which was only $200 up on the previous season.

Staying about the same for a long time, prices edged up to £27,402 and £27,952 for the pair of 2-litre UK grades as the 2007 season progressed. Coachwork colours for the UK included New Formula Red, Monza

Red Pearl, Deep Burgundy Metallic, Berlina Black, Moon Rock Grey Metallic, Platinum White Pearl, Silverstone Metallic, New Imola Orange Pearl, New Indy Yellow Pearl, Nürburgring Blue Metallic, Royal Navy Blue Pearl and Bermuda Blue Pearl.

As it happens, the Honda stand featured a Platinum White car with a red and black interior at the 2006 Paris Salon, bringing this elegant shade to people's notice in Europe. A limited edition of 50 'S2000 RJ' models was duly released soon after in France, Italy and Spain to celebrate Honda's F1 involvement, with Honda drivers Rubens Barrichello and Jenson Button signing the audio lid. Meanwhile, prices were carried over Down Under, with Deep Burgundy Pearl paintwork being added to the Aussie colour palette.

THE 2008 MY STATESIDE

First shown as a prototype at the New York Show in early April 2007, the S2000 CR (with CR standing for 'Club

Cover of the 2007 catalogue for the US market.

Racer') eventually went on sale in America in October, marketed as a 2008 model. According to Honda's John Mendel: "Open track days and club racing events have rapidly gained popularity as new racing venues and dedicated organisations make track time increasingly more attainable. The S2000 CR is designed as the ideal car to drive to the track, drive at the track, and drive home from the track with minimal fuss."

It was a proven formula, with the NR-A version of the Mazda MX-5 springing immediately to mind, but the timing was awful, of course, due to the fall-out following the Lehman Shock, meaning only 699 CR models would ever be sold in the US. That fact doesn't make the CR any less interesting to Honda fans; indeed, its relative rarity is another plus point for many in today's market ...

So what exactly is the S2000 CR? Well, starting with the obvious, the CR model was fitted with large aerodynamic appendages front and rear to reduce lift by as much as 80 per cent. The soft top was deleted, with colour-keyed fairings behind the seats (aping those of the 1950s Mercedes SLR to direct air to the rear spoiler) taking its place. While a hardtop was supplied with the car for inclement weather conditions, removal of the hood and its mechanism allowed more bracing in that area, leading to increased body rigidity and a significant reduction in weight when the hardtop was left off the car; sound deadening materials were also reduced, and the

Various views of the US-spec car for the 2007 season, including the dashboard.

An amazing view from the roof of Honda's US headquarters in California, with almost 500 S2000 owners turning up on 8 September 2007 for the chance to meet Uehara-san, and take a look at the new CR before it went on sale.

spare tyre and jack were replaced by a puncture kit in order to drop weight still further.

Ultimately, the CR was 45kg (99lb) lighter with the hardtop removed, or 23kg (51lb) lighter when it was on. For those who felt comfort was more important than speed, though, reinstating the air-conditioning and 120W radio/CD stereo system (delete options on the CR grade) took the car to within just 4kg (9lb) of the strict 2008 S2000; itself 4kg (9lb) heavier than before.

While there were no changes to the 2.2-litre engine and six-speed manual transmission, the CR model did adopt a sports exhaust to endow the car with a meatier, more sporting soundtrack. The ABS braking system (and VSA, for that matter) was left untouched, but stiffer suspension settings were a must for a car like this.

The springs were already seven per cent stiffer at the front and nine per cent stiffer at the rear on regular 2008 S2000s, but for the CR they were an additional 37 per cent stiffer up front, and 17 per cent stiffer than the latest strict S2000 at the back. Likewise, the damping force in the shocks was increased by ten per cent at the front and

five per cent at the rear for 2008 vehicles, with the CR going 50 per cent up on that at the front, and 32 per cent up at the rear end. Rounding off the suspension changes, a heavier 27.2mm (1.07in) anti-roll bar was adopted at the front of the strict S2000 at this time, but the CR bars were both uprated – 1.4mm (0.05in) and 1.1mm (0.04in) thicker, respectively.

The steering ratio was brought back to a quicker 2.4 turns lock-to-lock on the CR, with the rack featuring stronger mounts for greater steering accuracy, and stickier Bridgestone Potenza RE070 tyres were mounted on new, lighter 17in five-spoke alloys with wider 255/40 rubber at the back. Actually, the same wheels were adopted on the regular 2008 models, too, albeit painted a slightly lighter shade. For the record, in the case of the strict S2000, the 215/45 and 245/40 Potenza RE050 combination was retained, and rim sizes were still the familiar 7J and 8.5J widths for all cars.

Moving inside, the seats were trimmed in black suede-type cloth with yellow fabric inserts and yellow stitching. The predominantly black interior was lifted

US MARKET AP2 COLOUR AND TRIM OPTIONS

This sidebar charts the changes in the coachwork colour and interior trim for the US-spec S2000, with the date being the model year (MY) for Stateside vehicles. For the sake of completeness, notes on the Canadian market have been included, too.

2004 MY: New Formula Red, Berlina Black, Sebring Silver Metallic, Silverstone Metallic, Suzuka Blue Metallic (Nürburgring Blue in Japan), Rio Yellow Pearl (New Indy Yellow in Japan) and Grand Prix White paint choices. The red, black and yellow shades came with black leather trim only, the silver hues came with black or red/black leather trim choices, the blue paint was matched with blue leather trim only, and the white finish with tan leather trim only. The hood came in black, with a blue version offered as an accessory. As such, the US 2004 season colour and trim selection was much the same as that for 2003, with only the yellow shade changing. However, Canadian customers were restricted to Berlina Black, Sebring Silver Metallic, Rio Yellow Pearl and Grand Prix White paintwork options.

2005 MY: No changes, although Canada gained Silverstone Metallic paint to bring the coachwork choices up to five in that market.

2006 MY: Laguna Blue Pearl (Bermuda Blue in Japan) paintwork added, taking the body colour choices up to eight, and came with black leather trim only. Trim on white cars changed to black, and Sebring Silver cars lose red/black trim option (Silverstone Metallic options unchanged). No other changes, although Canada gained Moon Rock Metallic paint to bring the coachwork choices up to six in that market.

2007 MY: Sebring Silver Metallic and Suzuka Blue Metallic paintwork were dropped, and not replaced. Trim on white cars changed to red/black. No other changes, although Moon Rock Metallic dropped in Canada, and yellow replaced by New Imola Orange Pearl there, too.

2008 MY: For regular S2000 models, Chicane Silver Metallic (Synchro Silver in Japan) replaced Silverstone Metallic, with New Formula Red, Berlina Black, Laguna Blue Pearl, Rio Yellow Pearl and Grand Prix White completing the options. Apex Blue Pearl was added for the CR model only, joined by the black, yellow and white paint shades. While the CR came with black/yellow cloth trim only, a red leather option was brought back for regular black cars, augmenting the existing black leather trim, and regular silver cars continued with black or red trim choices. No other changes. In Canada, meanwhile, cars were offered in New Formula Red, Berlina Black, Chicane Silver Metallic, Apex Blue Pearl, Rio Yellow Pearl and Grand Prix White.

2009 MY: No changes, although Canadians found Grand Prix White replaced by a Platinum White Pearl shade in this final year.

---

by more yellow stitching on the suede door inlays and leather-wrapped steering wheel (still sporting cruise control switches), as well as the gearshift gaiter that dressed a new, spherical gearknob made from aluminium (shorter to reduce shift strokes still further). Carbon-fibre-style trim was adopted for the audio lid, and similar pieces were added to the console aft of the gearbox, too, along with a peak power indicator to the right of the speed read-out in the restyled dash panel.

For the first time in the US, the windscreen surround was finished in body colour, as per the other major markets. Even then, though, this rule of thumb only applied to the strict S2000 – the CR grade retained its black frame to better match the hardtop, which was always supplied in black on the sportier model.

As mentioned earlier, the strict S2000 inherited some revised spring, damper and anti-roll bar settings for 2008, subtly enhancing steering feel and high-speed stability, as well as some new five-spoke alloys. A tyre pressure monitoring system (TPMS) was added to the spec sheet for all 2008 cars, along with a CR-type instrument panel, with the fuel and temperature gauges now following the same arc as that of the tachometer (the strict S2000 had to do without the peak power indicator found on the CR model, though).

With a fresh colour palette accompanying the latest model, pricing for the 2008 season saw the strict S2000 listed at $34,300 (only $50 up on 2007) from 5 November, and the S2000 CR at $36,300 in basic guise. Putting back the air-conditioning and eight-speaker audio systems on the CR grade added an extra $1000, while all cars had a $670 delivery charge applied.

The S2000 CR as it appeared in New York, with and without the hardtop in place. The car would ultimately reach American showrooms in virtually identical guise to the prototype. Incidentally, the same wheels would be adopted across the board for 2008, albeit with a brighter finish on the strict S2000 model. Note also the unique black badging on the front wings, with a clear marker lamp lens next to it, rather than the usual amber item.

THE 2008 SEASON IN JAPAN

Launched at the 2007 Tokyo Show at the end of October, and known internally as the AP2-110 model, generally speaking, the 2008 JDM vehicles inherited the same chassis upgrades as the strict S2000 in America – new five-spoke alloy wheels, and revised settings on the springs, shocks and anti-roll bars. It's not quite that simple, though, for the 2008 season also brought with it the VSA system (including EBD and BA) for the first time in Japan, along with headrest speakers – something else new for domestic buyers. Strangely, whilst redesigned in the States, the old dashboard graphics were carried over for Japanese vehicles.

That notwithstanding, the biggest news concerned the loss of the S2000 Type V with its VGS steering, and its replacement in the line-up by the Type S – what amounted to a JDM version of the CR grade, albeit retaining the traditional soft top rather than the fairing behind the seats.

At 126,000 yen more than the regular model, the 3,990,000 yen Type S came with CR-type front and rear spoilers, underbody gaiters ahead of the wheels, darker Kaiser Silver paint on the alloys (but not wider tyres, incidentally), CR-spec suspension tuning, CR-type seats, door trim and gearknob, black wing badges, a black 'Type S' badge on the tail, and a puncture repair kit to replace

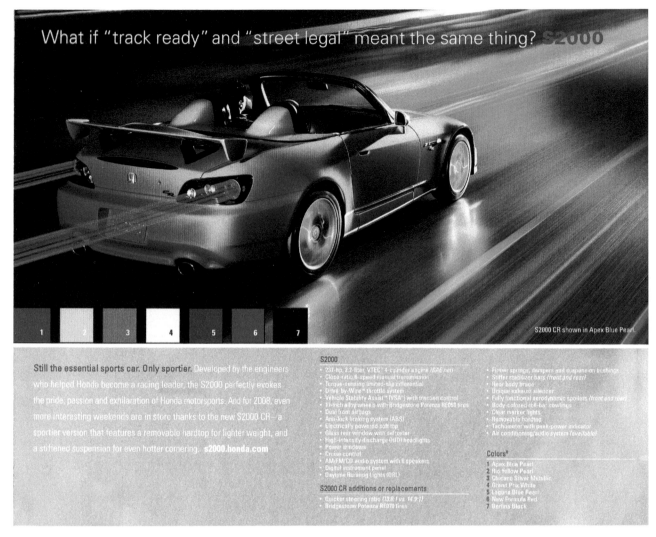

The S2000 section in the 2008 range catalogue for America, highlighting the new CR grade.

the spare wheel. For the record, the steering ratio was the same as that found on the strict S2000, as was the dashboard, steering wheel and gearshift gaiter. It really was a very good value package at the end of the day, but with a dark financial atmosphere hanging over Japan, sales would ultimately be restricted to 1755 units.

OTHER MARKETS IN 2008

The European cars for the 2008 season inherited the new wheels and suspension upgrades of the strict S2000 in America and Japan, but very little else was new in reality – even the dashboard was carried over, as in the domestic market. The coachwork colour choices were revised to include Berlina Black, Synchro Silver Metallic, Moon Rock Metallic, New Formula Red (aka Ascari Red), Platinum White Pearl, New Indy Yellow Pearl, and Bermuda Blue Pearl; leather trim came in either black, brown or red, the latter with contrasting black backs and sides to the seats.

The latest 2-litre car was priced at €39,590 in Germany, with a hardtop costing €2290 extra, metallic paint €590, and pearl paintwork €1490. In the UK, the strict S2000 was listed at £28,050, with the GT version commanding £28,600. Incidentally, at the end of November 2008, the familiar VAT rate of 17.5 per cent was reduced to 15 per cent for one year, adjusting the prices downwards slightly.

In Australia, the price of S2000 motoring went up by $1000 to $73,590. There were no Deep Burgundy or

(Continues page 148)

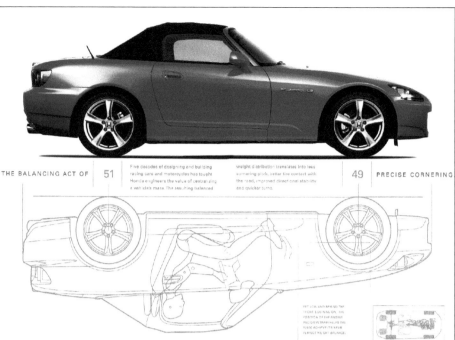

THE BALANCING ACT OF 51 | Five decades of designing and building racing cars and motorcycles has taught Honda engineers the value of centralizing a vehicle's mass. The resulting balanced | weight distribution translates into less cornering pitch, better tire contact with the road, improved directional stability and quicker turns. | 49 PRECISE CORNERING

The 2008 US catalogue may have looked completely different due to its new format, but in fact the contents were very similar, apart from the CR pages, that is. As such, with the New York Show car photographs and the other illustration from the range brochure, only the cover and two double-page spreads are really worth showing here.

The regular (strict) US-spec S2000 for the 2008 season. Note the new dashboard design for North American cars, and red seats having black back and side edges from now on.

そのダイナミズムは、
鷹栖ワインディングで育まれた。

リアルオープンスポーツ S2000の到達点として、走りを研ぎ澄ます。
鍛錬の舞台となったのは、そのワインディングの過酷さで
ドイツ・ニュルブルクリンクにも匹敵すると言われる、北海道・鷹栖プルービンググラウンド。
S2000誕生から、これまでの進化にいたるまで、数限りないテスト走行で
リアルオープンスポーツの走りを育んだ、S2000の「ゆりかご」とも言うべきコースである。
TYPE Sの開発にあたっては「鷹栖ワインディングベスト」を合い言葉に、
あくまでオープンにこだわりながら、従来のS2000を超えたアプローチによってダイナミズムを突き詰めた。
鷹栖の厳しいツインディングで、その潜在能力を引き出し、解き放ったTYPE S。
磨き抜かれたシャープな運動性と、いっそう軽快なクルマとの一体感を素肌で感じるのは、
鷹栖ワインディングだけではない。あなたとTYPE Sが駆け抜ける、すべてのシーンにそれはある。

S2000 TYPE S 登場

Cover and selected pages from the Japanese catalogue dated December 2007. One can see that red trim had black seat edges, as per America, but the brown leather option was left as a single colour, matched with black door panels on all cars. (continues overleaf)

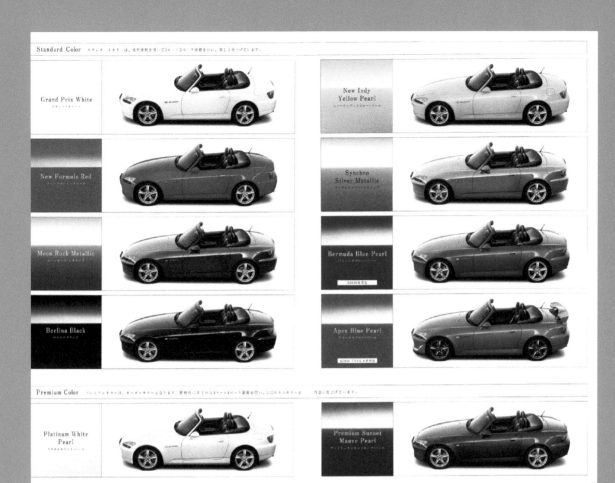

Grand Prix White

New Indy Yellow Pearl

New Formula Red

Synchro Silver Metallic

Moon Rock Metallic

Bermuda Blue Pearl

Berlina Black

Apex Blue Pearl

Premium Color

Platinum White Pearl

Premium Sunset Mauve Pearl

Seat & Interior Color

Dealer Option

Publicity photos of the new Type S model.

The Modulo catalogue covered all the items shown in the main brochure, plus a number of other interior trim items, illustrated here in the October 2007 edition.

Nürburgring Blue shades any more, but Apex Blue was added, and Synchro Silver Metallic replaced Silverstone Metallic. Things then stayed the same Down Under until the S2000 run came to an end in April 2009. With sales being hard to come by in the later years, with the 2-litre machine basically being shipped to order only, a grand total of 1818 cars were sold in Australia.

END OF THE ROAD

Like those in Japan, the cars sold in America for the 2009 season were exactly the same as those sold in the 2008 Model Year. Actually, that's not strictly true, for the price had increased by $695 across the S2000 line, and delivery costs had also gone up a little. Then, on 26 January 2009, came the shocking news via a press release: "2009 will be the final season for Honda S2000 production." Indeed, the S2000 wasn't listed in any 2010 material anywhere in the States. It just disappeared without ceremony ...

Takeo Fukui's time had also come to an end in February 2009, being replaced as Honda's President a few weeks later by Takanobu Ito, who'd joined the company back in 1978. In reality, few envied him the job during this incredibly difficult era for car manufacturers.

Although the initial schedules stated that S2000 production would end in June 2009, the axe was kept from falling a little while longer, and the last car was ultimately built on 7 August – all of the final batch being shipped to Europe to fulfil run-out orders of special editions.

Cover of the German catalogue dated November 2007.

A UK-registered GT model being pushed on the track ...

A 2008 S2000 for the British market. The yellow paintwork option was not available in Europe for the 2009 season.

Another UK S2000, this time with a view of the interior to go with it. Note the older style dashboard carried over on European cars.

2009 Honda
S2000

Indeed, Europe was about the only place where anything was happening on the S2000 front. For the 2009 season only, the Type S was sold in Germany, France, Austria, Holland, Italy, Belgium, Switzerland and Czechoslovakia (presumably to use up parts for the CR, which sold well under expectations due to the financial crisis), and then early March 2009 saw the official introduction of the so-called 'Ultimate Edition' model.

The 'Ultimate Edition' (actually sold as the 100-off £29,086 'GT Edition 100' in the UK) was given Grand Prix White paintwork with a matching hardtop, graphite-coloured wheels, red leather trim, a CR-type gearknob with red stitching on the gearlever gaiter, a numbered plaque on the sills (actually, the regular item with space made to take a four-digit number), and black wing badges.

As it happens, this was the first time Grand Prix White had been offered in the UK, making up for the loss of the Platinum White and Indy Yellow hues (as well as the brown trim option) on the regular S2000 line-up, which now commanded between £28,135 and £28,675 depending on the grade. The two-seater ultimately slipped from UK price lists at the end of October 2009, by which time a total of 7898 cars had been sold in the British Isles.

(Continues page 156)

Cover of the 2009 S2000 brochure for the US market. The contents were basically the same as those found in the downsized 2008 catalogue. Indeed, Honda's American arm got extremely good mileage from a lot of its photography.

The appearance of this Modulo concept car at the 2009 Tokyo Auto Salon, with its modified bodywork and interior, implied that all was well. However, it was announced that the S2000 was being dropped from the Honda line-up only a few days later ...

Cover of the last S2000 catalogue issued in the UK, dated February 2009. A lot of the photography was shared across Europe (with suitable retouching) for the 2008 and 2009 seasons.

A couple of pictures from the 2009 Geneva Show press pack, showing the tail and interior of the 'Ultimate Edition' model.

The UK version of the 'Ultimate Edition' was called the 'GT Edition 100.' Although supplied with a hardtop as part of the package, it has been removed in this series of shots showing details of the interior and engine as well as the exterior.

This S2000 was displayed at the 2020 Tokyo Auto Salon, sporting a fresh Honda Access front bumper moulding, a modified suspension, and a revised audio lid. While the chances of getting a totally new S2000 are still slim to non-existent, at least Honda has acknowledged the enduring appeal of the two-seater in its anniversary year.

Even that's not quite the end of the story, though, for the S2000 kept on cropping up at tuning shows on both sides of the Pacific amid frenzied rumours of a revival. Of course, history tells us that the revival never happened, and whether it will or not depends very much on the financial climate. Certainly, the American market would be well served by a convertible of the S2000's stature, but with the SUV as king and the horrific development costs involved in bringing a new car to the showrooms, life becomes increasingly difficult for enthusiastic engineers to get one past the beancounters. We'll just have to wait and see ...

Appendix
Sales & production figures

The official production figures – as supplied by Honda head office directly to the author – for the S2000 run, along with the yearly sales totals for the home (JDM) market, America and Europe (the latter being a vague area, but at least with the numbers coming from a trustworthy single source, they have consistency and meaning). Sadly, the figures cannot readily be broken down into model variations or types, and do not include prototypes ...

Year	Japan sales	USA sales	Europe sales	Total built
1999	7209	3400	1250	17,059
2000	3422	6797	3969	15,321
2001	1913	9682	2203	13,882
2002	1471	9684	2552	15,334
2003	961	7888	2105	11,088
2004	1087	7320	2164	10,415
2005	981	7780	1975	10,672
2006	1225	6271	1651	9328
2007	997	4302	1352	5913
2008	1228	2538	766	3581
2009	1122	795	647	1296
2010	42	85	19	0
2011	3	2	0	0
Total	**21,661**	**66,544**	**20,653**	**113,889**

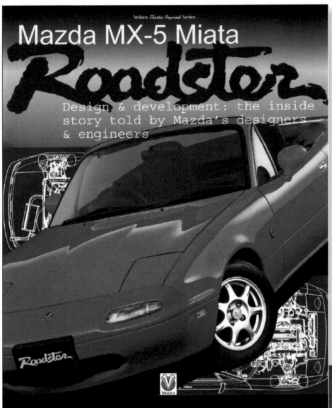
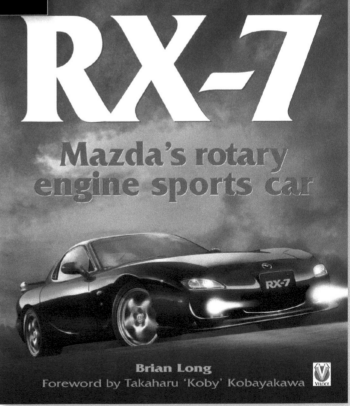

A milestone car, up there with the Toyota 2000GT, Datsun 240Z, and Mazda's RX-7 & MX-5. The first mid-engined production model to come from the Land of the Rising Sun will always have a special place in the hearts of all sports car enthusiasts. This is the definitive story, now updated to include the final years of production.

ISBN: 978-1-787110-62-5
Paperback • 25x20.7cm • 200 pages
• 396 colour and b&w pictures

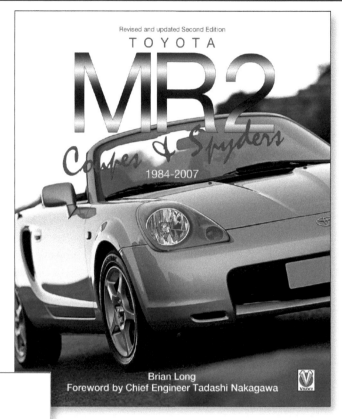

The Datsun 240Z inspired a generation of enthusiasts, outselling and outperforming almost all of its contemporaries. This book covers the full story of the Datsun sports cars, from the Fairlady roadsters through to the final 280ZX production model, illustrated throughout with contemporary material.

ISBN: 978-1-787115-25-5
Paperback • 25x20.7cm • 208 pages
• 298 pictures

INDEX

*The Honda company, its
products and subsidiaries
(including Acura) are
mentioned throughout this
book.*